W9-ATV-963

VIETNAM

PLACES AND HISTORY

STEWART, TABORI & CHANG
NEW YORK

Text
Paolo Rinaldi

Graphic Design
Anna Galliani

Editing Supervision
Valeria Manferto De Fabianis
Laura Accomazzo

Translation by
A.B.A. S.r.l.

Art Director
Patrizia Balocco

1 *Aromatic smoke rises from the incense burning in the Tam Son Hoi Quan Pagoda in the Cholon quarter.*

2–7 *A dragon, symbol of Vietnam, stands in the arch of the Gate of Humanity, one of the entry gates to Hue. In the background is Ngo Mon, the Midday Gate.*

3–6 *A view of Qui Nhon, capital of the province of Bin Dinh, which was heavily bombed during the war. Today it is a lively and popular vacation area.*

Copyright © 1998 White Star S.r.l.,
Via Sassone 22/24,
13100 Vercelli, Italy.

All Rights Reserved. No part of this pubication may be reproduced, stored in a retrieval system, or transmitted in any form or by any means, electronic, mechanical, photocopying, recording, or otherwise without written permission from the publisher.

Published in 1998 and distributed by
Stewart, Tabori & Chang,
a division of U.S. Media Holdings, Inc.
115 West 18th Street
New York, NY 10011

Distributed in Canada by
General Publishing Company Ltd.
30 Lesmill Road
Don Mills, Ontario, M3B 2T6, Canada

Library of Congress Catalog Card
Number: 97-68223

ISBN 1-55670-694-4

Printed in Italy

10 9 8 7 6 5 4 3 2 1
First Edition

CONTENTS

INTRODUCTION   PAGE   8
FINALLY AT PEACE   PAGE   20
HO CHI MINH CITY, VIETNAM'S
        ECONOMIC HEART   PAGE   54
THE ECSTATIC CHARM
        OF THE SOUTH-CENTER COAST   PAGE   74
THE TRIUMPH OF A LUXURIANT VEGETATION   PAGE   96
ETHNIC GROUPS AND TRADITION   PAGE 116
INDEX   PAGE 132

O nce upon a time, in the Far East, there was a dragon named Tonkin in the north and a princess called Cochin China in the south. They fell in love and had many children who fought one another in the Annam region in the center of Vietnam. When the children made peace, Vietnam was born. The dragon and the princess stand for the opposing forces yin and yang that, it is believed, govern the balance of the universe. Dragons have been a theme in Vietnam since time immemorial—in temples, on the roofs of houses, on chinaware, on silk garments, and nowadays on T-shirts, too. Vietnam itself is dragon-shaped: one eye is Ho Chi Minh City, the other is Hanoi, and Hue is the heart.

Vietnam occupies the easternmost tip of the Indochinese Peninsula; its

elongated, S-shaped territory is 1,025 miles long from north to south and a maximum of 372 miles wide, narrowing in the center to 31 miles wide. The country's shape is traditionally compared to the shape of the bamboo poles that the Vietnamese still use, especially in the countryside, to carry loads tied to each end. The country is bounded to the east by the South China Sea and has thousands of archipelagoes. It is divided into three geographical areas: Bac Bo (the north), Trung Bo (the central region), and Nam Bo (the south). These areas correspond to the administrative divisions introduced by the French: Tonkin in the north (Nam Ky), Annam in the center (Trung Ky), and Cochin China in the south (Bac Ky). Vietnam's mountainous north borders on China, and the center and south on Laos and Cambodia. The countryside of the huge Red River Delta in the north and the equally vast Mekong Delta in the south is exceptionally beautiful. Mountains and forests cover more than three-quarters of the country.

The country's climate is complex. Broadly speaking, it is cold in winter and hot in summer, but latitude and altitude cause wide variations to that norm, ranging from freezing cold winters in the mountains of the far north, to the year-round subequatorial heat in the Mekong Delta, to monsoon rains and violent typhoons in the coastal regions. There are also areas with a temperate climate,

8 top
The Lang Co Peninsula in the Da Nang region has miles of pristine beaches and a blue lagoon. The entire area has a promising future in tourism. During the war, Da Nang, which is Vietnam's fourth-largest city, had the biggest American military base in the country and hosted marines on leave from the front. Many American soldiers surfed at China Beach, which has been the site of recent world championship competitions.

8 bottom
South of Hanoi, at Hoa Lu, the capital of Dal Co Viet during the 10th and 11th centuries, are the remains of the temples of the kings of the Dinh and Le dynasties.

8–9 *Emerald green rice paddies in northern Vietnam, near the mountains in the Hoa Lu region. This city was the capital of the Dinh and Early Le dynasties. To the north the region is protected by natural barriers and has amazing caves.*

9 top
A sampan follows the flow of the current on the Perfumed River in the Hue region. The city is built on the banks of the river, 10 miles from the sea, and is the center of one of the country's richest archaeological areas. Buildings, mausoleums, tombs, and towers, constructed during the Nguyen dynasty, have been uncovered here.

including the Central Highlands, which occupy the southern part of the Truong Son or Annamite Range. In the south, the wet season runs from about March to November, with violent but short-lived downpours, and is followed by a dry season lasting from December to April. The lowest temperature recorded in Ho Chi Minh City is 44°F. Monsoons determine the atmospheric conditions in the central areas, but the storm seasons vary widely: In Nha Trang, the dry season lasts from June to October, while in Dalat it runs from December to March. A very fine drizzle known as "raindust" falls during the first few months of the year in the north, especially in Hanoi, where there are basically two seasons—a long winter and a long summer.

Tropical forests cover two-fifths of the country and contain many species that are now rare. Vietnam has 12,000 plant species, only 7,000 of which have been identified; 2,300 of them represent a source of food, fodder, wood for different uses, and medicinal plants. Land clearance for crops, the export of valuable wood (the country's third-largest source of hard-currency revenue), forest fires, and gathering of firewood have resulted in extensive deforestation in Vietnam; if it continues at the present rate, the forests will disappear in a few years, because even the extensive reforestation projects cannot keep up with the deforestation.

The forests contain 273 species of mammals, 773 species of birds, 180 species of relict fauna, 80 species of amphibians, hundreds of species of fish, and thousands of invertebrates. But the country's fauna resources risk extinction in the next decade, as has already happened with the tapir and the Sumatran rhinoceros, unless conservation programs are implemented. The greatest efforts thus far have been made on behalf of the largest species (bears, tigers, leopards, rhinos, and elephants); various types of bull, including the *ibanteng* (wild bull) and *koprey* (forest bull); and cobras, pythons, tortoises, crocodiles, peacocks, and deer. Two national parks already exist, both in the north (Cuc Phuong and Cat Ba, on the island of the same name), and 12 more are planned.

10–11 *The typical straw hat with conical crown is still in use, especially by women, who tie it on with a strip of cloth fastened at the throat.*

10 top left *An incredible quantity of merchandise can be transported by a* xe dap loi, *a cart pulled by a bicycle, common in the Mekong Delta area.*

10 top right *A view of peasant life still common in the countryside, where water buffalo do the heavy work.*

11 top *Characteristic facial features of the Vietnamese people are almond-shaped eyes, flattened noses, and thin lips.*

11 bottom *After the harvest, peppers and other vegetables are set out to dry in the sun in large, flat, round baskets that can often be seen along the roadside.*

12 top left
A brick-paved courtyard with stone statues precedes the tomb complex of the emperor Khai Dinh, one of the seven emperors of the Nguyen dynasty buried in the hills west of Hue.

12 bottom left
An extraordinary detail of a frieze in a Cham temple, depicting a procession of Hindu deities.

12 top right
A statue of a Hindu god, whose characteristics are mixed with Buddhist religious motifs.

12 bottom right
The Thien Mu Pagoda was built by the first emperor of Hue, Nguyen Hoang, between 1601 and 1613, on the left bank of the Perfumed River.

13 *A detail of a Cham statue displayed at the Cham Museum in Da Nang.*

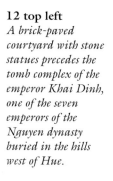

12

China

Tonkin

Gam

Lo

Hong-ha

Black da

Dien-Bien-Phu

Bac-Ninh

Hanoi

Haiphong

Do-Son

Cat-Ba

Ma

Laos

Gulf of
Tonkin

Phu Quoc Island

Thailand

Annamite Cordillera

Hué

Da Nang

Hoi An

Son My

Quang-Ngai

Annam

Song ba

Qui-Nhon

Cambodia

Nha Trang

Cam Ranh
Bay

Da Lat

Coinchin

Saigon

Golf of
Thailand

Ho Chi Mihn City
(Saigon)

Mekong

South China
Sea

Dao Phu
Quoc

Con Son

The Imperial City of Hue

The market in Hanoi

The mountains of southern Vietnam

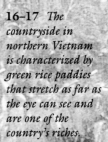
The floating houses on the Lan Ga River

16–17 The countryside in northern Vietnam is characterized by green rice paddies that stretch as far as the eye can see and are one of the country's riches.

18–19 Rice is a staple in the Vietnamese people's diet and is cultivated everywhere, even in the midst of these hills in the Son La area.

Along Bay

20 left
This elegant dancer from the 10th century is a splendid example of refined Cham art. It is on display at the Guimet Museum in Paris, where it was brought during the period of French domination.

20 right
This Cham bronze drum is on display in the Guimet Museum. In the 2nd century AD, the central portion of Vietnam belonged to the Champa kingdom, which battled the Khmers and Viets and drove the indigenous population farther and farther south, until dying out in the 15th century.

20–21 *This map of the Indochinese Peninsula was drawn by the Van Langren brothers in 1595.*

he birth of Vietnam is recounted in tales and legends in the National Annals of Vietnam. But the history of the lands that are now combined in a single nation began long before the legends; the oldest known human settlements in Vietnam date back to around half a million years ago. As a point of reference, the Bronze Age is dated at around the 13th century BC, at the time of the Dong So culture in Vietnam.

From the 1st to 6th centuries AD, the south of the country was part of the Funan kingdom, which had contacts with the Roman Empire, while the Champa kingdom, of Hindu origin, flourished in the vicinity of what is now Da Nang and extended even farther south in the 8th century. The Khmer ruled in the west, and the northern areas were occupied by the first Vietnamese people.

Vietnam was conquered on several occasions before the birth of Christ. In the 2nd century AD, the Chinese occupied the land on a permanent basis and tried to impose their culture on the local population. The efforts failed because of the native peoples' strong sense of national identity.

21 top
The drawing represents the Champa kingdom in the 14th century, according to Odoricus da Pordenone.

Chinese rule lasted for nearly a thousand years, and during that time the Chinese had to suppress at least 10 uprisings, with great loss of life, until the last in 939, when the Chinese troops were defeated at the Battle of the Bach Dang River. The battle marks the birth of a Vietnamese nation, although the new country was obliged to pay tributes to China every three years in exchange for its independence. The Ngo dynasty was the first of 14 dynasties that governed the country; the last, the Nguyen dynasty, ruled from 1802 to 1954.

22 bottom left
This drawing depicts Chinese Han invaders being driven out in March of the year 40. A major role was played by the Trung sisters. In the year 200 BC, before the country of Vietnam existed, the Chinese conquered the lands of Nam Viet, along the delta of the Red River. Trung Trac and Trung Nhi, the two heroines in the most famous episode of resistance, organized a revolt that forced the Chinese governor to flee. The sisters' reign lasted only three years, and China reconquered Nam Viet in 43 BC, but rather than surrender, the Trung sisters threw themselves in the waters of the Hat Giang River.

22 top left
A battle scene between Mongols and Chinese. It appears in the 1314 manuscript by Rashid al-Din entitled The History of the World, *on display at the National Library in Paris.*

23 This map of the
Indochinese
Peninsula by P. du
Val is dated 1686.
The history of the
French conquest of
Vietnam originally
did not involve
domination. The first
settlement was in the
central area of the
country in 1580, by
French missionaries
who came from the
Philippines. In 1615,
they were joined by
Jesuits who had been
expelled from Japan.

Vietnam was never entirely conquered, but despite the revolts and guerrilla activity, culture and the arts progressed under enlightened rulers: The Confucian Temple of Literature in Hanoi, where the Mandarins destined to govern the country took their degrees, was founded by the emperors of the Ly dynasty between 1010 and 1225. During the same period, the adoption of Buddhism was also promoted (the religion was destined to engage in a continual battle with Confucianism for supremacy), and the southern lands of the Chams were slowly conquered. The next dynasty, the Tran dynasty, ruled until 1400 and is noteworthy for its military victory against Kublai Khan and the diplomatic marriage of a Tran princess to a Champa king, a union that extended the country's territory through the peaceful annexation of the kingdom of Hue.

22 right
At one point,
Vietnam faced
Kublai Khan, shown
here, and in 1288
succeeded in stopping
him in an epic battle
on the Bach Dang
River.

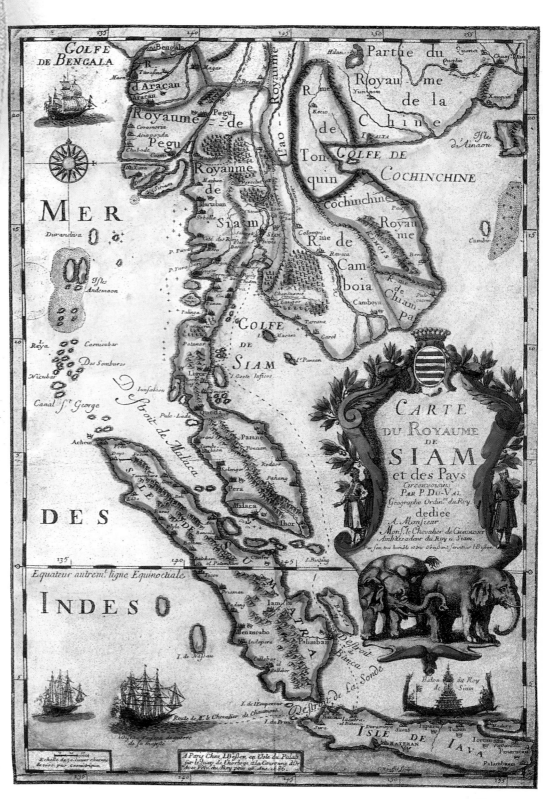

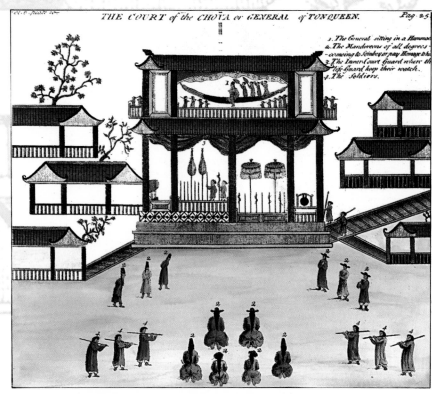

1. The General sitting in a Hammoc
2. The Mandereves of all degrees
   coming to Scombay or pay Homage to hi
3. The Inner Court Guard relieve the
   life Guard keep their watch.
4. The Soldiers.

24 top
The courtyard of the royal palace of Tonkin.

24 bottom
This map of Tonkin and Annam was drawn by the missionary Father Alexandre de Rhodes during the second half of the 16th century.

24–25 *A detail of Van Mieu, the Temple of Literature, built in 1070 by the Ly dynasty. Six years later, the School of the Nation's Elite, the first national Vietnamese university, was added. It was renamed the National College in 1235. Every three years, the competitive examinations for the title of court mandarin were held here. Much of the temple has now been restored.*

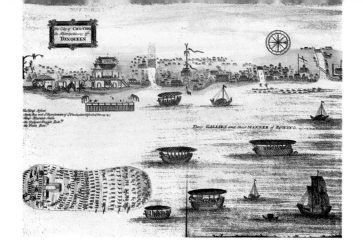

25 Hanoi in the 17th century, with the headquarters of the English and Dutch business agencies, when there were exactly 36 streets and 36 districts. This number began to increase in the 18th century, but the superstitious Vietnamese continue to disregard the change. Today Hanoi has at least 160 districts but continues to call itself Ba Muoi Sau Pho Phuong, the City of 36 Streets and 36 Districts.

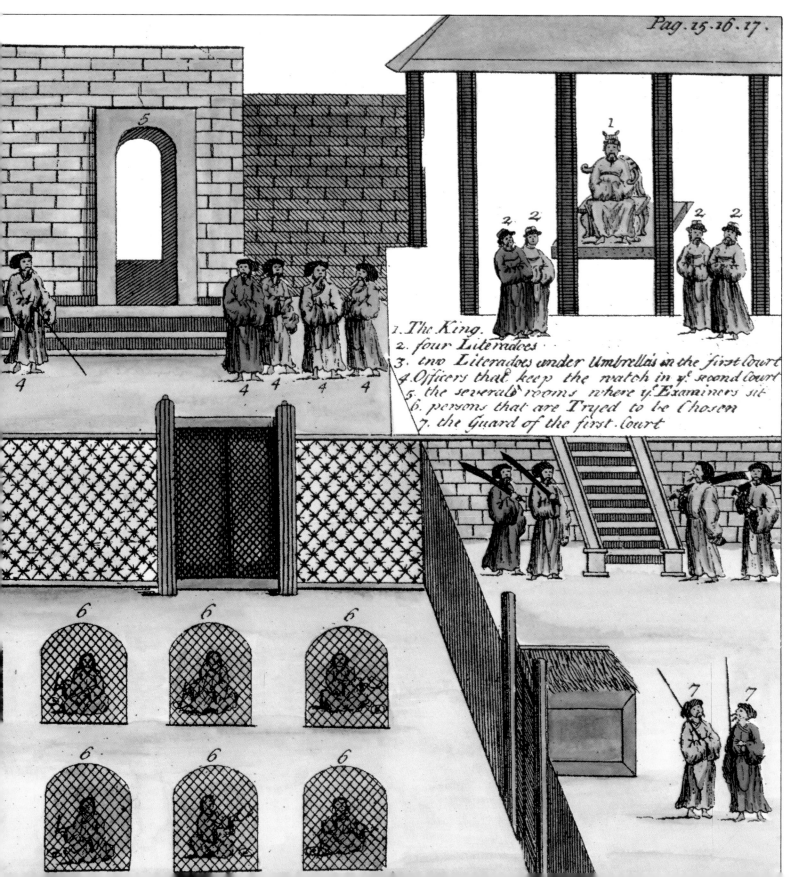

Pag. 15. 16. 17.

1. The King.
2. four Literadoes
3. two Literadoes under Umbrellas in the first Court
4. Officers that keep the watch in ye second Court
5. the several rooms where ye Examiners sit
6. persons that are Tryed to be Chosen
7. the Guard of the first Court

26 top left
This Belliard print shows Pierre Pigneau de Behaine, the bishop of Adran, who lived from 1741 to 1799. A missionary with the title of prince de Cochinchine, he was one of the principal architects of French power in Indochina

during the Nguyen dynasty's period of monarchic absolutism. He even succeeded in making the first conversion to Christianity by converting Cahn, a prince of the royal family and eldest son of Nguyen Anh.

A Chinese invasion in 1407 nearly ended Vietnam's independence, but stability was restored when a Le-dynasty prince liberated the country in 1428. The ensuing decades saw the alternation of periods of chaos with periods of prosperity and more internecine strife, until the country was divided along the Linh River on the 18th parallel in 1672. Fifty years later, a treaty brought about a form of peaceful coexistence between the two kingdoms, but it was not until the Nguyen dynasty (1792–1883) that unification was achieved by Nguyen Anh, with the aid of a French missionary, Monsignor Pigneau de Bahaine, bishop of Adran. The enterprising bishop was a skilled diplomat who arranged for military undertakings in exchange for territorial and trade concessions. When Nguyen Anh was crowned emperor with the name Gia Long in 1801, he named Hue the capital and built palaces, mausoleums, temples, and pagodas; passed new legislation; reorganized the government administration; and conquered and annexed Laos and Cambodia as vassal states. The name Vietnam dates from 1802, during Gia Long's rule, and is based on the names of the old lands. To change the country's name, Gia Long had to ask permission from the emperor of China, because Vietnam was still a subject nation. During the 19th century, two factions were fighting to gain power, and the Confucian pro-Chinese faction prevailed over the Christian pro-French faction.

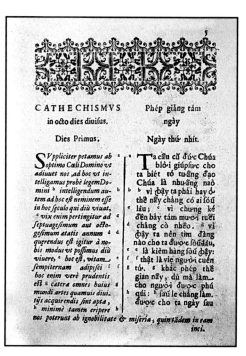

26 bottom left
In 1548, the missionary Father Alexandre de Rhodes Romanized the Vietnamese alphabet and wrote the first Vietnamese-Portuguese-Latin dictionary. The dictionary was printed in 1551 in a Latinized type of writing known as Quoc-Ngu, which came into common use a century later to replace Indian and Chinese script. Quoc-Ngu became obligatory after 1906 and was declared the national language in 1919, when the literary exams at the imperial city of Hue

were abolished. Today, senior citizens speak French, but the younger generation learn and speak English. Russian, which was introduced in the northern part of the country, is not used much now.

26 right
The first page of the Vietnamese catechism of Father Alexandre de Rhodes.

27 *This painting on display at the Vatican Missionary-Ethnological Museum shows the last judgment as interpreted by Vietnamese culture and symbolism.*

28–29 *An extraordinary pirogue race in Bassac, in Siamese Laos, an area under Thai influence. The pirogues are similar to those used in Bangkok in July 1996, during the magnificent celebrations of the 50th anniversary of the Thai king's reign.*

28 top *The costumes of southern Indochina, Annam, Cambodia, and Siam, set off on the banks of a river with an idyllic tropical landscape in the background, offer a peaceful image of a paradise lost that is more imaginary than real.*

29 top left
A camp in the Kengchan region, on the banks of the Mekong River near a rapid. The Mekong, or Cuu Long Gian (River of Nine Dragons), as it is called in Sino-Vietnamese, is one of the longest rivers in Asia, exactly 2,480,112 miles long.

29 top right
Many ethnic groups coexist in Vietnam. The country's ethnic populations include Vietnamese, Chinese, Cham, Khmer, and Indians. The country is also home to thousands of

Amerasians, the offspring of the American occupation during the war. The portrait of this young man, therefore, does not depict the various Vietnamese ethnic groups.

29 bottom right
A colored engraving of a family of epiphyte orchids, which cling to trees in damp areas. Despite the destruction wreaked in times of both war and peace, 12,000 plant species, only 7,000 of which have been identified, live in the forests of Vietnam.

**30–31 and
31 bottom**

These two engravings show a temple and a Saigon street. Today, Saigon's official name is Ho Chi Minh City, but many people still call it Saigon, its traditional name. All the old names and places of Saigon have changed, and the city has become the nerve center of the country. About a third of Vietnam's gross national product is produced here. During his travels in the past century, Mario Appelius noted in his book Yellow Asia *that bureaucratic Saigon was already building new palaces and new railroads. The same thing is happening now, but on a much larger scale. The war has become prehistory, as has the communist victory of April 30, 1975. Today, the historic hotels are no longer the meeting places they were during the years of French domination, and young people prefer Western-style bars.*

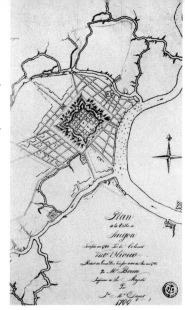

30 top
Ho Chi Minh City's Chinese districts have always played an important role in the city's history. In 1864, the Cholon quarter had 6,000 Chinese inhabitants and was separated from the city by one of the three rivers that cross it: the Saigon, the Nha Be, and the Long Tau.

31 top
This 19th-century engraving shows one of the many canals that connect the rivers that cross Ho Chi Minh City. Today, markets have sprung up along the canals, similar to those of the past. The most important in Cholon is the Binh Tay Market, and the

indoor Andong Market fills a four-story building, with a basement area full of cheap restaurants. If you want to admire the city from the Saigon River, you can rent a motorboat near the Saigon Floating Hotel and travel along the Ben Nghe Canal as far as Cholon.

32 *These period images depict some of the bloody battles during France's conquest of Indochina. Above is the Battle of Lang-Kep, on October 8, 1884. Below left is the taking of Son Tay on December 16–17, 1883, and below right is the French fleet bombing the* *coast. Following these victories, the French forced the emperor, Tu Duc, to cede the three western provinces of Cochin China, grant French missionaries free rein, turn over commercial ports, and pay a heavy fine. In 1867, Cochin China became a French colony, and between* *1872 and 1874 the citadel of Hanoi was conquered. But the French never achieved full control, and they battled various militias and the Black Flags, a semiautonomous army formed of Chinese troops and mountain tribes, during their tenure in Vietnam.*

In 1858, colonial occupation of Vietnam by the French began, and the situation escalated as the French took possession of Da Nang, Saigon, and finally the entire south of the country. In 1883, the French took control of the north, and the center became a protectorate. During the French colonial administration the north was called Tonkin, the center Annam, and the south Cochin China. Attempts by the French to modernize Vietnam

33 *This elegant, refined scene shows the conquest of Hong-Hoa by the French in August 1884. After the successes achieved by missionaries, especially during the* *Nguyen dynasty, France had lost almost all interest in the far-off country. It was only after the 1848 revolution and the advent of the Second Empire that* *colonization began in earnest. Saigon was conquered in 1859, and the era of French domination lasted until 1954.*

failed, partly because of the strict Confucian dogma that held sway in the country. The ill-fated revolts, revolutionary movements, and nationalist resistance movements failed just as miserably.

興化陣圖

33

Imprimé pour la
CHOCOLATERIE D'AIGUEBELLE
Monastère de la TRAPPE (Drôme)

34 top
*War in the Gulf of
Tonkin, as the
Vietnamese ambush
the French gunboat*
Mousqueton.

34 center
*The conquest of the
citadel of Hanoi by
the French army,
commanded by
Captain Henri
Rivière. Years before,
another navy
captain, Francis
Garnier, conquered
the city to restore
order after Jean
Dupuis illegally
established himself
there between 1872
and 1874 to trade
with the troops of a
general who
controlled the
Yunnan River. Once
he occupied the
citadel, Garnier
demanded tribute
from the fortresses on
the Red River. He
was killed by the
Black Flags.*

34 bottom
*A group photo of the
allied French-Chinese
command stationed
at Tonkin during the
signing of the peace
treaty on June 9,
1885.*

34–35 *The death of
Captain Henri
Rivière in 1883
following an ambush.
The captain's head
was carried from
village to village.*

35 top
The taking of Saigon in early 1859. After complications following the conquest of Da Nang, plague, and lack of support from Catholic allies, the French left only a garrison in the city and moved south, following the monsoon. They reached Saigon and conquered it.

From 1904, Vietnam was involved in a series of events that were closely linked to the French and international events: the Japanese victory over Russia, agreements with Japan and then China, attempts to solve the independence issue by diplomatic means (which were always opposed by Paris), and the Russian Revolution, which had a great influence on a young revolutionary later known as Ho Chi Minh. Ho, who took part in the Versailles Conference in 1919, went to Moscow in 1922 and embraced the cause of Stalin, and was sent to China as a delegate in 1924. There, Ho made contact with Vietnamese delegates and founded an association for the liberation of the country in the same year as the death of the emperor, Khai Dinh, and the ascent to the throne of his son, Bao Dai, who was sent by the French to study in France until 1932.

36 top
This amateur 1887 photograph bears the following handwritten inscription on the back: "An execution in Tonkin." The crowd attending the event includes people in Western dress wearing helmets and Vietnamese, recognizable primarily by their conical hats, either *worn on their heads or tied around their necks and hanging down their backs, as is still the fashion in the countryside today.*

36 center
The same photo album contains this photo showing cruel treatment of prisoners, who were forced to carry a sort of pillory made of bamboo poles.

37 bottom left
An official ceremony in 1930, with the young emperor, Bao Dai, attending. He ascended the throne in 1925 when he was 12 years old and still a student at a school in France. He died in 1997.

37 top right
The emperor, Khai Dinh, and the heir to the throne, Bao Dai, nine years old at the time, in Paris, paying homage to the Unknown Soldier in 1922.

37 bottom right
This photo, taken between 1902 and 1905, documents the custom of French officials to grant audiences to Vietnamese dignitaries in official residences. This is the commander of the Cao Bang territory in the Tonkin region. Note the beauty of the typical French turn-of-the-century colonial buildings.

36 bottom
A squadron of Tonkinese machine-gunners stands in double file. This is a classic image of the Vietnamese resistance to colonialism and a testimony to the errors made by the French, whose policies caused the impoverishment of the local population, until this region finally lost its economic importance for French industry. As far as the French were concerned, colonialism was good for making quick profits, not long-term investments. Colonial rulers exploited mineral resources or built tea, coffee, and rubber plantations that paid miserable wages to workers who were subjected to inhumane treatment. Newspapers reported that between 1917 and 1944, of the 45,000 contract workers in a Michelin rubber plantation, 12,000 died from disease and malnutrition.

37 top left
This photo of the terrace of the Grand-Hotel de la Rotonde shows the pleasant life of the colonists. At sunset, officials, diplomats, civil servants, and women in corsets and crinolines crowded the terraces and cafés decorated with large mirrors and ornamental stucco. They played bridge, discussed the latest edition of the Courrier de Saigon, *and sipped glasses of absinthe under the great fans, sheltered from the oppressive heat, the crowds of coolies, and the danger of malaria. They watched new passengers arrive, exhausted by their long voyage aboard the steamships of the Messageries Maritimes. They attended the Municipal Theater and religious functions in the cathedral, had their accounts at the main office of the Banque de l'Indochinie, and shopped in the elegant boutiques on rue Catinat.*

38 left
Ho Chi Minh's given name was Nguyen That Thanh. He was born in the village of Kim-Lien on May 19, 1890. His father
was a government official who was stripped of authority because of his anti-French activities. The family's ardent nationalism and the
local revolutionary tradition played a decisive role in the future of young Ho Chi Minh.

38 top right
Ho Chi Minh and his generals examine strategic plans for the Battle of Dien Bien Phu. Many events in the life of Ho Chi
Minh are obscure, both because of his clandestine activities and because he used at least 15 different names during his lifetime.

The Indochinese Communist Party was founded in 1930, and two opposing factions immediately emerged: one pro-Chinese, and the other pro-Russian. Revolts and uprisings continued until the outbreak of World War II, when the situation was complicated by the invasion of France. The Vichy government accepted the Japanese occupation of Indochina and tried to retain control of Vietnam, but the Japanese ousted the French.

During the same period, the Vietnam Independence League, known as the Vietminh, was founded in China by Nguyen That Thanh, better known as Ho Chi

38 bottom right
Ho Chi Minh reading a newspaper. After attending secondary school in Vin and Hue, Ho worked as a cook aboard a French ship. The beginning of World War I found him in London, but by 1917 he was in Paris under the name of Nguyen Ai Quoc and was affiliated with the French Socialist Party. In 1919, he unsuccessfully participated in the Versailles Peace Conference, broke with the Socialist Party, and became one of the founders of the French Communist Party. He published a monthly magazine entitled Le Paria *("The Pariah"). In 1922, he participated in the fourth Comintern*
Congress in Moscow. He left France in 1923 to move to Moscow, where he attended university and wrote French Colonization on Trial. *He was sent to China as a Comintern agent in 1924. In Canton, he organized the Revolutionary Youth Association of Vietnam, but Chiang Kai-shek's break with the Communist Party forced him to return to Moscow in 1927. Two years later he was in Thailand, and in 1929, he was invited to Hong Kong, where he founded the Indochinese Communist Party. He was arrested in 1931. Upon his release in 1932, he went first to Amoy and Shanghai, and then returned to Moscow in 1934. In 1938, he returned to*
China and in 1941 created the Vietnam Independence League, the Vietminh. Imprisoned again in 1942, this time by the Chinese, he was freed by promising to unify the Vietnamese against the Japanese. At this point he began using the name of Ho Chi Minh, which means "he who illuminates." In 1945, the Vietminh controlled northern Tonkin, and after the defeat of the Japanese, Ho Chi Minh filled the political void, occupied Hanoi, and on September 2 founded the Democratic Republic of Vietnam, of which he was elected president.

39 bottom right
Ngo Dinh Diem, born in 1901, proclaimed himself president of the South in 1955 and breached the Geneva Accords, which provided for free elections throughout the country. Diem's government was a family dictatorship: One brother was a bishop and another was a police chief who boasted of personally torturing political prisoners. Madame Nhu, the president's wife, was also noted for her scandalous lifestyle. After eight years of peace, in 1960 the Vietnam drama once again exploded onto the world scene, with images of Buddhist monks immolating themselves as a protest against Diem's corrupt dictatorship. The United States responded to the crisis by sending 20,000 "military advisors" to guide Diem. Students and Buddhist clergy revolted against Diem, and the CIA and the American embassy finally decided to eliminate him and his family. In 1963, Diem was found assassinated in a church in which he had sought refuge.

Minh. The Vietminh's rise to power was long and difficult. But on September 2, 1945, the Democratic Republic of Vietnam was proclaimed, elections were held, and France was forced to recognize Vietnam's independence.

The ensuing bombing of Haiphong by the French triggered the war of independence that lasted 10 years and constituted the most confused period in contemporary Vietnamese history. The Vietminh troops were commanded by General Vo Nguyen Giap, and the war strategy consisted mainly of sabotage actions. China aided the young republic with military hardware and supplies, and South Vietnam came under strong pressure in 1954. When Dien Bien Phu fell on May 8, the French troops retreated below the 16th parallel.

At this point the United States, fearing what was then known as the "domino effect" of communist expansion, decided to support the French and Bao Dai's regime. When Bao Dai was subsequently

39 top left
A meeting with colonels René Cogny and Bigeard, who were involved in the Castor Operation during the war in Indochina. The war ended in 1954 with the victory of the Vietminh and the division of Vietnam into a communist north and a noncommunist south.

39 top right
A group of Vietminh prisoners forced to march to the Dien Bien Phu concentration camp.

40 center
Bicycles bringing reinforcements to the front during the Battle of Dien Bien Phu.

40 bottom
A tragic moment during the Battle of Dien Bien Phu. In October 1945, General de Gaulle ordered his admirals to reestablish French sovereignty over Indochina. In one month the expeditionary force occupied Cochin China and reached an agreement with the Vietminh that provided for French occupation for five years. But the French promptly violated the treaty. While Ho Chi Minh was in Paris for the ratification, in Saigon the French proclaimed the Republic of Cochin China on June 1, 1946. On November 23, following an incident they had provoked, the French fleet bombed the port of Haiphong in a retaliatory attack and caused the death of 6,000 civilians. Ho Chi Minh launched an appeal for a national uprising.

40 top
A scene from the Battle of Dien Bien Phu, which put an end to the Indochinese war in 1954. It is difficult to calculate the exact number of years of war that Vietnam had to bear. Apart from the years of French occupation, one could begin either in 1941, when the guerrilla war against the Japanese invaders began (the French, who had occupied the whole region since 1859, surrendered to Japanese troops), or in 1945, when the Paris government tried to take back the colony. In any event, these decades involved entire generations, with only brief interludes of peace. On August 6, 1945, after the surrender of the Japanese, Vietnam seemed to have secured its independence. The so-called Night Club Emperor, the weak collaborator Bao Dai, was forced to abdicate, and on September 2, the Republic of Vietnam was proclaimed in Hanoi.

41 bottom
The flag of North Vietnam flying over the Dien Bien Phu battleground. In July 1954, in the presence of the great powers in Geneva, the French and the Vietminh signed the peace treaty. France abandoned Indochina forever, Laos and Cambodia became independent, and Vietnam was divided in two. The peace treaty, which was not signed by the United States, provided for unification within two years, at which time the people of the south, who had remained within the Western orbit, would decide whether they wanted to rejoin the communist North. But the elections never took place, and Vietnam remained divided. The war in Indochina cost the French 100,000 lives.

41 top
A row of Vietminh cannons opens fire on the fortress of Dien Bien Phu.

41 center
The advance of the Vietminh was unstoppable. Dien Bien Phu fell in 1954, the same year the French were defeated. Vo Nguyen Giap, a former history professor who became a head of the liberation army and a great strategist, stated this motto: "If the enemy is strong, avoid him. If he is weak, attack him." The French at first succeeded in holding the large cities, but guerrilla attacks intensified in the countryside, to the advantage of the Vietminh. Cao Bang and Dong Khe were among the first towns along National Highway 4 to fall. When the French army was exhausted, the fortress of Dien Bien Phu, which was considered impregnable, surrendered. Twelve thousand French died during the siege and 1,000 more were taken prisoner.

deposed, the dynasty ended forever, and Ngo Dinh Diem became president of the new Republic of South Vietnam.

The end of the war was officially declared on July 20, 1954. The Geneva Accords, signed the following August, called for a general election to be held two years later and divided the country in half along the 17th parallel. But Diem never called the election, and the Buddhist

42 top right
Ho Chi Minh visiting North Vietnamese troops after the Battle of Dien Bien Phu.

42 bottom right
A car parades through the streets of Saigon, crammed with soldiers and decorated with banners announcing the victory over the French.

42 top left and center
Two rare and dramatic photos taken during the surrender, as French soldiers who survived the Battle of Dien Bien Phu, their arms raised, approach the victorious troops of the Vietminh.

42 bottom left
Immediately after the battle and the surrender of the fortress of Dien Bien Phu, the approximately 10,000 surviving French (at least 12,000 died during the siege) were gathered into a makeshift camp.

43 top right
Armed, perfectly trained Vietminh soldiers parade in Hanoi.

43 right center and bottom right
The protest of Buddhist monks against the Diem government reached its height with

public immolations. This photo shows the fiery suicide of the venerable Tich Quang Duc.

43 top left
The third National Workers' Congress of Vietnam was held in 1960. Standing and dressed in Chinese-style civilian clothes, President Ho Chi Minh speaks into the microphone.

43 bottom left
People took to the streets in Saigon during the visit of the International Control Commission on July 23, 1955. The photo shows the vehicles of commission representatives set on fire along with Hotel Majestic furniture, which had been thrown out of the windows.

monks made a stand against his regime; many immolated themselves in protest, including 66-year-old Tich Quang Duc on June 11, 1963. The advance of the northern communists (now known as the Vietcong) continued, and the Vietcong extensively infiltrated the southern territory. Diem was assassinated in 1963 during the first of a series of coups d'état that culminated in the election of General Nguyen Van Thieu in 1967.

44 top
John F. Kennedy, photographed on September 28, 1962, during a press conference, was the first U.S. president to become involved in what would become known as the "dirty war."

American involvement in South Vietnam began in the early 1950s and increased considerably under the Kennedy administration. United States Army personnel acting in South Vietnam were limited to a role of "military advisors." The war became one of the central issues in the 1964 U.S. presidential election. Republican candidate Barry Goldwater was a fervent supporter of intervention against the communists. His opponent, "peace candidate" Lyndon B. Johnson, won the election but deepened U.S. involvement in the war against North Vietnam, a war that the United States never officially declared.

Johnson used incidents in the Gulf of Tonkin, some real and some fictitious, to justify his involvement in Vietnam's affairs. He ordered the first air strike against North Vietnam in 1964, after Congress voted almost unanimously in favor of the Gulf of Tonkin Resolution, which gave Johnson carte blanche to handle military operations in Vietnam.

In March 1965, the first combat troops disembarked at Da Nang. A year later, 385,300 U.S. troops were stationed in Vietnam and 6,644 had been killed. The death toll rose quickly. The United States implemented various strategies and plans: pacification of villages; mobile "search and destroy" units; forced

44 bottom left
Lyndon B. Johnson was responsible for the escalation of U.S. involvement, which officially began on August 2, 1964, when the U.S. destroyer Maddox was attacked in the Gulf of Tonkin by North Vietnamese patrol boats. Johnson ordered a reprisal that destroyed and sank 20 patrol boats. Later, the Pentagon revealed that the Maddox was participating in sabotage operations with South Vietnam

ships along the North Vietnam coast. By August 5, 1964, President Johnson had obtained permission from Congress to use U.S. armed forces to maintain the peace in Asia and the southeast.

44 bottom right
Richard Nixon, who succeeded Johnson in 1969, was the last U.S. president involved in the Vietnam War and was primarily responsible for restoring peace.

45 top right
One of the many meetings between Le Duc Tho and Henry Kissinger. Nixon promised peace in his presidential platform, and as soon as he was elected, he began negotiations, which were almost always held in Paris, *often in great secrecy. Ho Chi Minh died in 1969, and in 1970, the conflict extended to Cambodia, where the pro-American general Lon Nol came to power after driving out Prince Sihanouk.*

45 bottom
A meeting in the Party Military Office to examine the course of battles underway in Ho Chi Minh's campaign for the liberation of Saigon. The second from the left is General Tran Va Tra, and the man holding the baton in his hand is General De Giapon.

45 top left
This 1965 photograph shows General Westmoreland, a commander of the U.S. forces in Vietnam. By 1965, the United States had embarked on the most tragic adventure in its history. Senator Morse, one of the few members of Congress who opposed the war, commented, "We have given the president the power to fight a war without a declaration of war." But 85% of Americans approved the escalation of U.S. involvement, the bombings, and the sending of troops. American generals believed it would take 50,000 men to liquidate the Vietcong, but by the end of the war, there were 500,000 U.S. soldiers fighting in Vietnam. The Vietcong resisted with the unofficial aid of Moscow and Peking. The war was fought with napalm, defoliants, and B52s that bombed Hanoi, Haiphong, villages, and rice paddies.

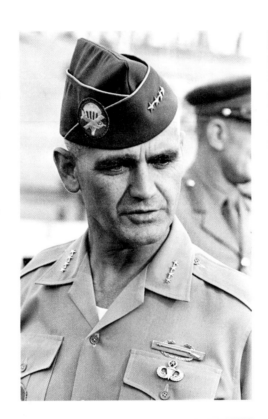

evacuation of villages; scientific destruction in "fire at will" areas; and "Operation Phoenix," which was designed to eliminate Vietcong leaders. But none of these operations was any more than a partial success.

In January 1968, the Vietcong launched the Tet Offensive in a hundred towns, including Saigon. The attack was preceded by diversionary attacks elsewhere. Although taken by surprise, the United States and the South Vietnamese retaliated viciously. Only Hue managed to hold out for 25 days; all the other towns occupied by the Vietcong capitulated after two or three days. The Tet Offensive had widespread repercussions in the United States, where

46 top left
This photo, dated January 8, 1968, shows an armed Vietnamese woman in the Hai Bac area in North Vietnam.

46 bottom left
The transport of South Vietnamese troops from the Khe San area to Laos in American helicopters.

46 right
An American soldier on patrol in South Vietnam shoots napalm grenades into the forest, where groups of Vietcong are presumably hiding. By 1968, American

public opinion about the war had changed. Hundreds of thousands of young people joined protest marches in Washington. Draftees burned their draft cards in front of the Pentagon. Protesters coined the slogan "Make love not war." The protest extended from American universities throughout the Western world. Vietnam's turmoil spared no one. The war extended far beyond the battlefield, inflicted brutal wounds on the land and people of Indochina, profoundly lacerated the United States, and shook the democracies of Europe, which staggered under the violent tremors of revolt during the harshest and most dramatic phase of the Vietnam war. The Indochinese popular earthquake, with its long aftershocks, produced the psychological and political upheavals that shook Europe and the West during the late 1960s and early 1970s.

antiwar demonstrations took place, especially on university campuses. In the wake of the events, General Westmoreland, commander of the armed forces in Vietnam, was relieved of command; Lyndon Johnson decided not to stand for reelection; and Richard Nixon was elected president.

Despite Nixon's plan to end the war, the conflict escalated again in 1969. But that same year, peace talks began in Paris between Henry Kissinger and Le Duc Tho, his North Vietnamese counterpart. The bombing of Cambodia triggered further protest marches in the United States, and four demonstrators were killed by the National Guard during a demonstration at Kent State University in Ohio. In 1971, the scandal of the Pentagon Papers broke: Secret documents published by the *New York Times* proved that the military and former presidents lied to Congress about the reasons for the intervention in Vietnam.

47 top
A boat patrol, with heavy support weapons from the River Marines Flotilla, moving slowly along the banks of the canals in the Mekong River Delta in search of hidden Vietcong troops.

47 center
Women, senior citizens, and children prepared Molotov cocktails. This undated photograph could have been taken in any of a thousand similar villages at any time during the war.

47 bottom
Photographed from the back, these American soldiers during a routine mop-up operation seem frightened of the unknown forces hiding in the forests in front of them.

The North Vietnamese offensive in 1972 triggered retaliatory bombing of Hanoi and Haiphong. But on January 27, 1973, an agreement was reached at the Paris talks. A resolution prohibiting further U.S. military involvement in Vietnam was passed by Congress and scheduled to take effect on August 15, 1973. Richard Nixon was reelected in the meantime, but he was implicated in the Watergate affair shortly after the election and forced to resign in 1974.

In January 1975, the North Vietnamese army crossed the 17th parallel in breach of the Paris Accords and launched what was to prove a decisive attack against an enemy that had been ordered to retreat. The capitulation of South Vietnam was signed on April 30, 1975, in the Independence Hall at Saigon, now renamed the Unification Hall.

After the fall of South Vietnam, the few Americans still in Vietnam were evacuated from the roof of the American Embassy at the last minute and airlifted by helicopter to ships anchored off the coast. One hundred thirty-five thousand Vietnamese also left the country, and half a million more followed them in the five years

48 top
This famous, brutal photo bears the date of February 1, 1968, and shows the execution of a Vietcong officer by a South Vietnamese policeman named Nguyen Ngoc Loan. In recent years, an American journalist found the policeman in the photo. He was working in or the owner of a Chinese restaurant in Los Angeles, California.

48 bottom
A U.S. soldier lying prostrate over the body of one of his fellow soldiers. The photograph was taken on May 2, 1967, in the area of Khe San on the Laotian border.

after the surrender. Many refugees also headed in the opposite direction. South Vietnamese exiles who returned home were persecuted because they were considered to have been corrupted by their stay in the United States.

Figures published after the fighting ended indicated that nearly 3 million Americans took part in the Vietnamese conflict in various capacities, and 58,175 men and eight women were either killed or listed as missing in action—more than twice the lives lost in the Korean War. According to the official figures, the U.S. military commitment cost $165 million (compared to $18 million for the Korean war); 15 million tons of munitions were used; and 3,689

49 *This 1965 photo is a searing testimony to the horrors of war; a civilian shows a group of South Vietnamese soldiers the small body of his son, who was killed by the Vietcong in a village in South Vietnam near the Cambodian border. American intellectuals launched fierce resistance to the war in Vietnam, even as early as the escalation of February 7, 1965. On May 21 and 22 of that year, student groups organized a committee at the University of California, Berkeley. Norman Mailer and others went to Berkeley to speak, and Bertrand Russell sent a recording. The speeches were published in the book* We Accuse. *Civil disobedience and non-violence were the moral pillars of the march in Oakland, near San Francisco, on October 10, 1965. The theme of the war entered literature with a vengeance, and intellectuals began to go to Vietnam, invited by the Committee for Vietnam Peace; they included journalists from the* New York Times *and writers Susan Sontag and Mary McCarthy, who was sent by the* New York Review of Books.

aircraft and 4,857 helicopters were destroyed. The South Vietnamese army lost 223,748 men. Estimates of the losses on the other side were probably too low: North Vietnamese and Vietcong casualties are estimated at 440,000 killed and 1 million wounded. But the greatest losses took place among the civilian population, which was literally decimated by the conflict—4 million lives were lost. Two thousand Americans and 300,000 Vietnamese are still listed as missing.

The period that followed the war was one of power struggles; oppression; demands; political repression; economic disasters; compulsory agricultural collectivization; purges of

50 top
In March 1975, the South Vietnam National Liberation Front captured Hue, the ancient imperial capital, which had already been seriously damaged during the Tet Offensive in 1968. On March 11, two weeks earlier, Banmethuot, the strategic stronghold of the Central Highlands, was captured. It was a winning move that stopped the south's military forces in their tracks.

50 bottom
This picture, taken near the stadium and dated July 5, 1967, was photographed almost 10 years before the one above and shows the devastation caused by the U.S. bombardments of Hanoi.

51 top
*U.S. and South
Vietnamese troops
retook the city of Hue,
which had been
conquered by the
Vietcong during the
Tet Offensive. This
photo is dated March
3, but it would be
another 10 days
before the city finally
fell.*

51 bottom
*A U.S. soldier runs
from a burning hut,
carrying two children
with him. No one has
been able to provide
anything more than
an approximation of
the number of
civilian lives lost in
North and South
Vietnam in a war
that affected
everyone,
methodically
destroying even the
smallest villages
scattered in the
countryside and
along the rice paddies.*

intellectuals, executives, religious leaders, and even children; and anti-capitalist campaigns against Chinese property.

Because of the political unrest, many Vietnamese fled their country. The odyssey of the boat people is all too well known, and the fate of those who took refuge in Hong Kong now rests with China, which regained possession of the island in 1997.

In 1979, Vietnamese troops intervened in Cambodia against the Khmer Rouge, allies of the Chinese. Yet another invasion of Vietnam by China in retaliation lasted only 17 days. The Khmer Rouge continued its guerrilla activity for 10 more years, until Vietnam withdrew its troops from Cambodia in 1989.

52 top left
The first tank of the South Vietnam National Liberation Front entering the courtyard of the Presidential Palace on the morning of April 30, 1975. The palace had been abandoned six days earlier by the head of state, Van Thieu. General Van Tieng Dung, the right hand of the legendary Vo Nguyen Giap, had been in command of the communist forces since February 5.

52 bottom left
The unstoppable advance of the tanks of the Liberation Front. This photograph was taken in Bien Hoa on April 30, 1975, shortly before the tanks entered Saigon. The American ambassador, Graham Martin, held out until March 29, then a helicopter took him, with the American flag rolled up under his arm, to the aircraft carrier Blue Ridge, *which was anchored in the China Sea. The event marked the end of the war, although an illusory armistice had already been signed in Paris on*

January 27, 1973. The agreement was supposed to have guaranteed an end to the hostilities, maintained peace in the country, and guaranteed national fundamental rights as well as the right of the South Vietnamese people to self-determination. The Hanoi government used it to better prepare its decisive attack, exploiting both American disorientation after Nixon's resignation in the Watergate scandal and Congress's decision to send additional military assistance to South Vietnam.

The treaty that formally put an end to the hostilities was signed in 1992. After the signing, a period of peace finally began for Vietnam.

More than 20 years after the end of the war, military huts still surround Ho Chi Minh City's airport, and although the helicopters in the hangars do not fly now, they are said to be still armed with missiles. The last U.S. citizens left Vietnam on April 25, 1975, and trade and diplomatic relations between Vietnam and the United States resumed in 1995, when the United States revoked its embargo and opened a diplomatic office in Hanoi.

Recently, the winds of *do moi*, the local version of perestroika, have been blowing in Vietnam. Today, foreign aid has been liberalized, and tourist visas are issued on a routine basis.

52 right
Tan Son Nhat Airport on April 30.

53 top left
Crowds in front of the Presidential Palace on the day of the fall, or liberation, as many journalists called it, of the capital of South Vietnam.

53 bottom left
The People's Liberation Front is welcomed with banners that may indicate political movements, with portraits of Ho Chi Minh. Unfortunately, after taking over South Vietnam in the name of victorious and just national unity, the North

Vietnamese tried to inflict their hegemony on the entire former Indochina, while the people, exhausted by hunger and repression, fled on makeshift boats headed for distant shores. The tragedy of the boat people, especially those interned in Hong Kong, has still not been resolved.

53 top right
A tank and soldiers of the National Liberation Front fraternize with the crowds in front of the Presidential Palace.

53 bottom right
Welcome the men of the Liberation Front. A new era was beginning for the unified country, an era that was supposed to be happy but was not. Northern ideologues believed they could introduce real socialism to the people of the delta. After April 30, 1975, the steely northerners

descended on the south and decreed the end of private property. Revolutionary struggle was merciless, although not as bloody as in neighboring Cambodia. The result was repression, gulags, epidemics, prison, and hunger. Finally, in 1991, the government was forced to approve a decree that maintained nominal ownership of

the land by the state, but granted peasants the private use of the land they worked, the right to assign land to third parties, and a life estate to their children, an essential condition in a country where the family is everything. It was the return of private property.

HO CHI MINH CITY, VIETNAM'S ECONOMIC HEART

55 center
The Thong Nhat (Reunification) Conference Hall is a modern building built by the old regime in 1966. It is now a museum.

55 bottom
A few automobiles, many mopeds and motorcycles, and the traditional bicycles in the chaotic traffic in Ho Chi Minh City.

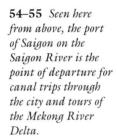

54–55 *Seen here from above, the port of Saigon on the Saigon River is the point of departure for canal trips through the city and tours of the Mekong River Delta.*

54 top left
The creativity of the Vietnamese people, who have a special flair for decorative arts, is expressed in daily activities, religious festivals, and even the simple display of flowers at the People's Central Market.

54 top right
Three beautiful girls at the Flower Market in Ho Chi Minh City pose in their traditional ao dai *costumes of solid-colored silk. The outfit consists of pants and a tunic with slits on the sides.*

55 top
The modern city has grown up along the river. This channel is known as Song Sai Gon.

H o Chi Minh City is the name of this city, but residents still call it Saigon. Whatever its name, the city already looks ultramodern; it is here that economic change, with its wide-ranging social repercussions, is most evident.

Traffic is chaotic in Ho Chi Minh City. There are not many cars on the road, but there are millions of mopeds and bicycles. Ho Chi Minh City has a population of at least 3 million and is frenetic, dynamic, and vivacious. It has wide boulevards, large squares, elegant buildings, numerous parks, and an attractive layout. The roads are lined with shops, kiosks, stalls, and hawkers displaying their wares on the pavement. You can buy absolutely anything here, from sweet-and-sour soup to the most sophisticated electronic equipment.

Some of the city's districts still retain a French flavor, and croissants as good as any in Paris are to be had in some cafés. Other districts clearly imitate the small-town American architecture of the 1960s. The General Post Office building is green and white. In the famous street of shops and big hotels, once known as rue Catinat and now called Dong Khoi, you can find antique furniture and caviar, old French and American clocks and war souvenirs, both real and imitation. Also available are models of helicopters and fighter planes that a child started making

with "imperialist" soft-drink cans; the industry now occupies his entire family. The models cost a dollar and are on sale in the shop and on the pavement in the corner opposite the Rex Hotel, a big hotel converted from a two-story garage in 1961. The building looks like a hideous apartment building by day, but it sparkles with lights by night. The

56 bottom left
The first of the two former U.S. embassies, which was bombarded by the Vietcong in 1967 and is now transformed into a dormitory for

banking students. The second former embassy is the one from whose roof the last U.S. citizens in Vietnam were evacuated on April 30, 1975.

56 right
The Post Office in Ho Chi Minh City was built by the French during the early 20th century.

56 top left
The Saigon Floating Hotel is one of the most exclusive hotels in Ho Chi Minh City. Originally anchored along the coast of northern Australia, the hotel was bought by a Vietnamese entrepreneur, who made his fortune with this five-star floating hotel.

hotel's decor verges on kitsch (there's a Mona Lisa painted on the huge bamboo curtain that hangs in the dining room), and the building has a terrace where guests sip their aperitifs. The Continental, another large hotel, was the headquarters of the international press during the war. The city's only five-star accommodation is the Floating Hotel, a ship fitted out as a hotel.

To the west of District 1, the traditional Saigon visited by Western tourists, is District 5, the Chinese quarter called Cholon, which means "big market." This Chinatown, once inhabited solely by Chinese, suffered the consequences of a vicious campaign against capitalism and foreigners in 1978. As a result of the campaign, most residents were forced to leave. The refugees are now returning, bringing cash and business skills with them, and the hotels of Cholon are once again filling up with Chinese-speaking businessmen who now control the finance, gold, and trade of the city.

There are numerous places of worship in Ho Chi Minh City, including the Giac Lam Pagoda

56-57 *A modern area of the Chinese quarter of Ho Chi Minh City, with modern, multistory houses, and posters. Building construction is booming and is changing the face of many quarters of the city.*

57 top *The bilingual advertising for a U.S. soft drink at the Flower Market is a clear indication that times have changed.*

58 bottom right
A nighttime view of a balloon vendor and the famous Hotel Rex, which, along with the Hotel Continental, housed war correspondents during the conflict. Today, the two hotels are meeting places for businessmen. Most of the action in Graham Greene's novel The Quiet American *takes place in the Hotel Continental.*

59 *A number of junks sail slowly along the tranquil waters of a canal in Ho Chi Minh City, a city built on three rivers and thousands of canals. The three rivers are the Saigon, the Nha Be, and the Long Tau. Boats are available for rent at Me Ling Square at the end of Hai Ba Tung Street. The ferries that cross the Saigon River also leave from the square.*

58 left
The large Binh Tay Market is the most important and crowded market in the Cholon quarter. The market is about a block away from the Cholon administrative district.

58 top right *The xich lo is cheap, provides good views of the city, and is the most popular means of transportation in the city. This is Yersin Street, where there is a market.*

58 center right *Ben Nghe Restaurant, on the banks of the Saigon River. The city offers all kinds of entertainment at night, including dancing, karaoke clubs, and water puppet shows, a Vietnamese speciality with puppets that are skillfully manipulated on the surface of a tank of water.*

61 top right
The Xa Loi Pagoda in Ho Chi Minh City, built in 1956, conserves a relic of the Buddha and is famous for having

played a central role in the opposition to the Diem regime. In 1963, the pagoda was sacked and all its monks arrested.

62–63 *The faithful light sticks of incense to celebrate the Tet Festival, the first day of the year according*

to the Buddhist calendar, in the Thien Hau Pagoda in Ho Chi Minh's Cholon quarter.

60–61 *The Buddhist pagoda of Vinh Nghiem, built in Japanese style in 1973, is the newest and largest in Ho Chi Minh City. The photograph shows the outer park, the entry to the religious enclosure (to the left), and the upper floors of the religious building.*

61 top left
Outside the Vinh Nghiem Pagoda, the faithful light traditional votive incense.

61 bottom left
A ceremony outside the Xa Loi Pagoda, which became a special devotional center after the fall of the old regime.

(considered the oldest in the city, although it was rebuilt in 1900), which retains the 18th-century layout and many of the original decorations. The prayers that are held at the pagoda every day are accompanied by chants, drums, bells, and gongs and follow a ritual that has fallen into disuse elsewhere. The Giac Vien Pagoda is equally venerated. A third pagoda, the Taoist pagoda of the Jade Emperor, contains statues of spectral divinities and grotesque heroes shrouded in a pungent mist of incense. Some of the city's modern pagodas have towers up to 10 stories high. The impressive neo-romanesque redbrick Notre Dame Cathedral has two square towers 131 feet tall. It's worth climbing to the top of the bell tower

of Cho Quan Church for the breathtaking view. The Xa Loi Pagoda is the place where opposition to Ngo Dinh Diem's regime began; the Hindu temple of Mariamman is like a piece of southern India transplanted into the heart of Ho Chi Minh City; and the lovely blue-and-white central mosque is an oasis of peace amid the din of the city. Also noteworthy are at least 10 more outstanding

64 top left
*The National History
Museum, built by the
French in 1927,
documents the
development of the
various Vietnamese
cultures. The museum
is located in the
Botanical and
Zoological Gardens,
which offer a refuge
for anyone trying to
escape the chaotic
traffic in the
downtown area.*

64 center left
*City Hall was built
by the French and is
now home to the
People's Committee of
Ho Chi Minh City.*

64 bottom left
*Several statues of
the Buddha in the
National History
Museum, once called
the Museum of the
Republic of Vietnam.*

64 top right
*The Ho Chi Minh
Museum, located in
an old customs
building, contains
many personal effects
of "Uncle Ho." The
exile of Ho Chi Minh
began in this
building, when in
1911 he left Vietnam
to work as a cook on a
French mercantile
ship.*

pagodas in the Cholon district; the Church of Cha Tam, the last refuge of the dictator Diem; and a mosque with an attractive *mihrab* (prayer niche).

The War Crimes Museum, once known as the American War Crimes Museum, has a new name, but the brochure handed out at the door explicitly refers to crimes committed by the American imperialists during the war of aggression against Vietnam. The pictures on display in the museum are horrifying. The courtyard displays armored vehicles, munitions, bombs, and weaponry alongside a French guillotine, the tiger cages in which Vietcong prisoners were incarcerated, and a kiosk selling American lighters, bullets, and old Art Deco watches.

A visit to the Museum of the Revolution, housed in a neoclassical building dating from 1886, is a must for those interested in the Vietnamese people's struggle for liberation. The basement has a labyrinth of fortified bunkers and reinforced concrete corridors with living areas, a kitchen, and a conference room that served as a temporary hiding place for President Diem and his brother in 1963.

The development of Vietnamese cultures is explored in the History Museum through a valuable collection of objects. The quaint Ho Chi Minh Museum displays some of Ho's clothes, his Zenith radio, and other memorabilia and is housed in

an old customs house, from which Ho Chi Minh left the country in 1911 when he worked as a cook on a French ship.

Another noteworthy Ho Chi Minh City attraction is a restaurant called the Binh Soup Shop, which was the Vietcong headquarters in 1968. The Unification Hall, also known as the Independence Hall or Presidential Palace, is an outstanding example of 1960s architecture. The building's spacious rooms are beautifully decorated with the most exquisite products of modern Vietnamese craftsmanship. Less attractive are the two concrete-faced former U.S. embassies. Both buildings have been converted to other purposes—one is a student residence hall, and the other houses the offices of a government agency.

65 *This statue of the Buddha is in the National History Museum. At the back of the building is a library that holds a large collection of books from the French period.*

66 right
This statue depicts a standing Buddha. Buddhism, Confucianism (originally a system of social and political ethics), Taoism (created as an esoteric philosophy for the erudite), and

Christianity are the four great philosophies or religions that have fused with popular belief and animism to create what is known as the triple religion, or Tam Giao.

66 right
A bronze statue of a Hindu deity from the Cham period. The Champa rulers were Hindu and built the world's first religious sanctuaries,

such as the temple built at My Son in the 4th century. The god-king Shiva was represented in the form of a phallic lingam, a symbol of creation.

67 top left
This lacquered statue is done in Chinese style. The Chinese dominated Vietnam for centuries and influenced artistic expression, cultural and intellectual life, language, and traditions in Vietnam. Before the country adopted Latin characters, even Vietnamese writing was based on Chinese ideograms.

In addition to the Chinese market in Cholon, there are the Ben Thanh, Bin Thay, and Andong markets. Fans of military surplus can visit the army surplus market of Dan Sinh, where bulletproof jackets are in great demand.

67 bottom left
This statue of Confucius, like all the others shown in these pages, is in the National History Museum.

67 right
A sculpted stone bust of a deity from the Cham period. The Cham governed the central part of Vietnam for centuries but have now become a minority.

AROUND
HO CHI MINH CITY
AND THE SOUTH

68-69 *The delta region is still inhabited mostly by Khmer Krom, a people of Chinese, Cham, Khmer, and Vietnamese origin who follow various religious doctrines.*

69 top left
There are numerous floating markets in the Mekong Delta area, like this one in Cai Rang near Cantho.

69 top right
A woman from the Mekong Delta wears the typical conical straw hat, held on by a ribbon tied at her throat.

68 top
A dense network of canals and about a hundred ferries connect the nine provinces of the Mekong Delta.

68 bottom
Fishermen use large square nets along the canals of the Mekong Delta. The delta is formed by various tributaries and branches of the river that flows down from Tibet, passing through various countries.

Places to visit near Ho Chi Minh City include Cu Chi, the underground city of tunnels and passages excavated for thousands of miles, and the Caodaist Tay Ninh Temple, already described in the chapter on religions. The Black Goddess Mountain is a place of pilgrimage, and there are many resorts on the South China Sea with luxury hotels, thousands of cheap boardinghouses, and numerous massage parlors. The most famous resort is the Vung Tau Peninsula, which the French called Cap Saint Jacques. The area seems fated to turn into the Vietnamese answer to Thailand's Pattaya.

Off the coast is the seldom-visited Con Dao Archipelago, called Poulo Condore in Europeanized Malaysian (originally Pulau Kundur). The archipelago was used as a penal colony by the British, the French, and the Diem government.

The huge Mekong Delta, the southernmost region of Vietnam, is an alluvial plain that advances 259 feet a year. Except in the mangrove swamps, the soil is very fertile and intensively cultivated. The delta is the granary of the country and also supplies coconuts, sugarcane, fruit, and seafood. The Mekong River, which originates in the Tibetan highlands and is 27,900 miles long, splits into two main branches and various smaller offshoots before flowing into the South China Sea.

The road north crosses the Dong Noi district, passing an interminable succession of churches with gigantic religious decorations, shops with tidily arranged goods, TV antennas on bamboo poles, and tobacco laid out to dry on straw mats. The road is good and climbs gently up to the Central Highlands, which occupy the southern part of the Annamite Range, where ethnolinguistic minorities known as Montagnards live. There are at least 33 different ethnic groups in this area, and the

70 top
A number of ships lie at anchor in the South China Sea, not far from the sculpted rocks of the Hon Chong Peninsula.

70 bottom
To fish and move from one boat to another, fishermen from the delta—this is in Phan Tiet—use baskets waterproofed with pitch.

people from these groups are often encountered at the markets dressed in the traditional costume of their own group. The women carry their babies on their backs, wrapped in a long strip of cloth that is passed over the mother's shoulders and tied at her waist.

Apart from Lam Dong Province (where Dalat is situated), the Central Highlands were off-limits to tourists until a few years ago, because the secret reeducation camps so much talked about in the West were located here. Today, the police occasionally hassle tourists, perhaps by demanding payment of nonexistent taxes. The Dalat highlands supply South Vietnam's markets with tea, coffee, tobacco, poinsettias, cabbages, potatoes, and other produce.

Dalat, about 60 miles from Ho Chi Minh City, is the city of eternal spring. It was founded in 1893 and used to be called "Little Paris." Wealthy French families spent their summer holidays in Dalat, and the last Vietnamese emperor lived here between 1949 and 1955. The tops of the hills are covered with conifers, and the large, eclectic villas, some made of exposed stone or half-timbered, are reminiscent of buildings in Brittany and Normandy. Karaoke is popular in the chalet-style cafés, and there is a semicircular central market at the end of a square, not large but very well stocked. The roadside stalls

70–71 *A woman completely submerged in wicker and straw baskets tied together.*

71 top *The river that divides Cu Chi, between beaches and rice fields, cuts through luxuriant vegetation.*

72-73 *Forests and waterways surround the lake that laps the city of Dalat, in the Central Highlands northeast of Ho Chi Minh City.*

72 top left *Dalat as seen from the lake. Because of its excellent climate, the city is a vacation area for Ho Chi Minh City's foreign residents, and the houses reflect every style of French architecture.*

72 top right *The great Xuan Hoang Lake skirts the golf course built by the French and runs through a large part of the city. Here you can rent horses for pleasant rides in natural surroundings.*

73 left *This woman is wearing the typical conical hat. She was photographed in the Dalat Market in the Central Highlands, one of the richest trading centers in Vietnam.*

73 top right *No visit to Dalat and the province of Lam Dong is complete without seeing at least one of the many waterfalls, like this one at Prenn, which tumbles down 49 feet from a cave that can be reached by a little bridge.*

73 center *The still waters of Dalat's Lake Xuan Huong mirror the white clouds, low hills, villas, and surrounding pine groves.*

serve good food, especially the dishes made with fresh vegetables, mouthwatering fruit (apples are called *bom,* a corruption of the French pomme), strawberry jam, dried black currants, candied peaches and plums, cranberry jelly, artichoke tea, avocado ice cream, and soya and ginger mousse.

Curiosities in Dalat include a 3-mile-long rack railway (it used to reach the coast but was closed in 1964 after Vietcong attacks and never reopened); the House of a Hundred Roofs, also called the House in the Forest or the Forest in the House, an unusual building on the lakeside; and the flower gardens and greenhouses in which

hydrangeas, fuchsias, and orchids are grown.

Outside Dalat there's an amusement park that also has shops and a riding school with instructors dressed as cowboys. This area is still called the Valley of Love, but it has now lost the peaceful characteristics it once had. The Valley of Love also has numerous pagodas, churches, and a convent.

The area around Dalat has streams, lakes, waterfalls, and famous caves. The Pren Caves are the most attractive and always crowded; the Lien Khang, Gougah, and Pongour caves are quieter, but you must hire a guide to visit them.

74–75 *Fishermen repair their nets on the shore of Nha Trang.*

74 top left
A beautiful beach of golden sand near Nha Trang.

74 top right
U.S. marines used to surf at the famous beach in the Da Nang region. In recent years, this area has hosted world surfing championships.

75 top
You can admire this extraordinary coastal landscape from Cloud Hill, a pass 4,000 feet high and next to another mountain known as Bach Ma, or White Horse.

75 bottom
The Lang Co Peninsula, one of the most beautiful coastal areas of the country, extends out to the blue sea.

T his area, which was once part of the Champa kingdom, is still inhabited by the Muslim Cham people and contains a wealth of relics of their civilization, including Po Klong Garai, a complex of four 14th-century towers resembling Hindu temples, complete with the bull Nandin and lingams (stylized phalluses symbolizing fertility). A speciality of the local cuisine is roast gecko with mango. The coast is famous for its beaches, and the U.S. soldiers called it "Vietnamese Hawaii." The loveliest bay, Cam Rahn, is still partly occupied by Russian military bases, but it is destined to become another popular holiday resort. The bay lies a few miles from the town of Nha Trang, which has the loveliest town beach in central Vietnam. But there are clear signs that organized prostitution is developing in Nha Trang. As you explore the country, you will find that even the worst characteristics of Thailand are being imitated in Vietnam.

It takes five hours to travel by bus from Nha Trang to Qui Nhon, through rice fields and rocky coasts with white beaches on the blue China Sea. Some 16 miles north of Qui Nhon are the ruins of the ancient Cham capital, Cha Ban. On the way to Hoi An, is Son My, or My Lai, where the infamous massacre took place. You must obtain a permit from the Quang Ngai police to visit it.

In beautiful Hoi An, known as Faifo by Western merchants in ancient times, Portuguese, Chinese, French, and Japanese influences are intermingled. Vietnamese ships once set sail for the neighboring countries from this port, which was built at the same time as Macao and Malacca. Silk, china, cotton, lacquer, and medicines are for sale here, in the streets adjacent to the covered Japanese bridge, in districts that have

76–77 *The Cham temple complex of Po Klong Garai, built around 1307 on Mount Betel. The entry to the main tower houses a statue of a dancing Shiva, while in the interior is a statue of the bull Nandin, to whom peasants make votive offerings.*

76 top left
The panoramic view includes the Cham towers of Po Nagar, just a few miles from Nha Trang.

76 top right
The ruins of My Son are near Da Nang, the center of Cham civilization for many centuries.

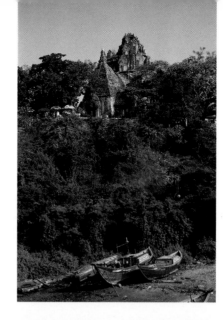

not changed for a century and a half; the ironwood houses are particularly interesting and can sometimes be visited for a small fee.

Hoi An has a magnificent architectural heritage, and at least 844 buildings are listed as being of historical interest. The listed buildings are classified in nine categories: shops; pagodas; Vietnamese and Chinese temples; communal buildings; Chinese meeting halls; tombs of various religions; ancestor worship chapels; bridges; and wells. The buildings are often traditional structures that are rarely to be found in the rest of the country. Some particularly interesting features on the structures are the roofs, with concave and convex tiles laid alternately, in accordance with the rule of yin and yang; the shop doors, which are surmounted by circles; and the courtyards with outer staircases.

Hoi An was the first town to accept Christianity. The missionaries who preached here in the 17th century included Frenchman Alexandre de Rhodes, who invented Quoc-Ngu, the Roman alphabet that replaced ideograms of Chinese origin and is still used to write Vietnamese today.

77 top
My Son was chosen by King Bhadravaman as a religious sanctuary. Starting in the 4th century, many temples were built in this area.

77 bottom
The altar of the Cham temple of Po Nagar, near Nha Trang, with lavish offerings of flowers and fruit to a deity of Hindu origin.

78–79 *A sampan plies the waters of the Thu Bon River, on the banks of which, 3 miles from the coast, is the city of Hoi An, once a flourishing trading port and meeting place for Oriental and Western culture under the Nguyen dynasty.*

78 top left
This covered, arched bridge was built in the 17th century by the Japanese community of Hoi An.

78 top right
This building in the French quarter of Hoi An was built when the city had an important port at the mouth of the river. But the river silted up, so maritime

traffic was ultimately blocked. In 1980, UNESCO approved a project for the classification, protection, and restoration of the monuments of Hoi An.

79 top
The Chua Phuk Kien Pagoda was built in Hoi An in the 18th century by the Chinese community, which came from Fukien. Beautiful, cosmopolitan Hoi

An's population included Chinese, Japanese, Dutch, English, and French. Hoi An also received Vietnam's first Italian, French, and Portuguese missionaries.

79 bottom
The interior of the Chua Phuk Kien Pagoda. The altar is dedicated to Lady Thien Hau, the goddess of the sea.

80–81 *The boats in the port of Nha Trang are blue and edged with red. Nha Trang is one of Vietnam's major tourism centers.*

81 top
This photograph of a family on a colorful motorcycle was taken in the village of Buon Me Thuot in the Nha Trang region.

81 center
A bread vendor in the market of Da Nang. Known to the French as Tourane, the provincial capital has now become the fourth-largest city in Vietnam.

81 bottom
A military helicopter in a square in Da Nang, which suffered great damage during the war.

82 *These sinuous rock sculptures are displayed at the Da Nang Museum.*

83 top left
This statue, in the Da Nang Museum, depicts the god Shiva.

83 bottom left
A detail of an 11th-century frieze from the province of Quang Nam-Da Nang showing a dancing female figure.

83 top right
A unique bronze statue from the Uma culture is displayed at the Da Nang Museum.

83 bottom right
Gajasimba, the elephant-lion, comes from the Bin Dinh Province, a city in the Champa realm conquered by the Vietnamese in 1470. The works displayed at the museum date from between the 7th and 15th centuries and were found in various areas, most of them in the province of Quang Nam-Da Nang.

84 top
The extraordinary Cave of the Buddha in the Marble Mountains near Da Nang.

84 center
Highway 1 connects the southern part of the country to the north and has an elongated form similar to the silhouette of a dragon.

84 bottom
A natural arch in the Marble Mountains, or Mountains of the Five Elements (metal, water, wood, fire, and earth), which are about 5 miles south of Da Nang.

84–85 *The Marble Mountains were originally five islands, which gradually became part of the mainland as the waters silted up.*

86 top
The entry gate to the tomb of the emperor Minh Mang, located where the two tributaries of the Perfumed River meet. Minh Mang built the imperial city, but his mausoleum was completed by his successor, Thieu Tri, in 1843.

86 bottom
This stern stone warrior stands guard at the mausoleum of Minh Mang.

86–87 *The sampan traffic is chaotic on the stretch of the Perfumed River that passes through central Hue, the ancient capital of the Nguyen sovereigns, located 7 miles from the coast.*

87 top left
The wide courtyard of the mausoleum of Minh Mang, with the emperor's tomb in the center.

87 top right
A brief stretch of the Perfumed River, along the banks of which the city

of Hue was founded and gradually developed over time. The tombs of seven of the 13 emperors who reigned until their deaths are located in the more peaceful valleys of the hills that surround this city.

At the foot of Cloud Hill, the mountain pass overlooking the South China Sea, across which the road climbs to the north, lies Da Nang, the town that the French called Tourane, with white beaches, a coastline embroidered with coves, and spurs of rock emerging like icebergs from the emerald green bay. This is where the U.S. marines disembarked on March 8, 1965.

They were welcomed on the beach by Vietnamese girls with garlands of flowers and placards reading "Welcome to the gallant Marines."

Da Nang is now a lively, carefree town with shops, tailors, and dance halls. Reasonably priced tablecloths, embroidery, and silk can be purchased from the Catholic nuns in the cathedral. You will find a ripe apple in your hotel room to welcome you. The town is of no particular interest apart from shopping, but the surrounding area offers a wealth of beautiful landscapes like the Marble Mountains, Cloud Hill, Bai Non Nuoc (which the Americans called China Beach), the Cham towers of My Son, the mountain resort of Ba Na, and Lang Co Beach.

In town, there are pagodas, temples, cathedrals, and the tombs of French and Spanish soldiers, but the main attraction is an elegant peristyle building, erected in 1915 by the École Française d'Extrême Orient, that houses the largest collection of Cham sculptures in the world. The museum is somewhat chaotic but displays outstanding stone sculptures, sometimes in an attractive setting, from the period between the 7th and 15th centuries.

Hue, 682 miles from Ho Chi Minh City, is reached by crossing the Hai Van or Cloud Hill Pass, from which there is a magnificent view over the Lang Co Peninsula, with strips of sand shaded by coconut

88–89 *The statues of military mandarins in the courtyard of the mausoleum of Khai Dinh stand guard over the tomb of the emperor, the adoptive father of Bao Dai, who reigned for nine years during the colonial period.*

88 top left *The mausoleum of Tu Duc was begun in 1864 and completed in three years, with the help of 3,000 laborers.*

89 top right *The tomb of the emperor Khai Dinh is made of stone and reinforced cement. It took 11 years to build the mausoleum, from 1920 to 1931.*

89 top

This banquet pavilion is within the enclosure of the mausoleum of Tu Duc, the fourth emperor of the Nguyen dynasty, who reigned for 36 years and was able to enjoy the magnificent area chosen for his mortal remains while he was still alive.

palms and lapped by the transparent waters of turquoise lagoons. In the mountains is the resort of Ba Na, where, until World War II, French vacationers were carried on litters up the last 12 miles of the path.

Another more famous path, the Ho Chi Minh Trail, can be seen near the mountain town of Gian. The "trail" consists of a series of routes cross the Truong Son mountain range and the western part of Laos. Numerous permits are required to visit the area.

The ruins of the most important archaeological site in the Champa kingdom are in the area, at My Son.

Hue, the ancient capital of Annam, was the political capital from 1802 to 1945. It was the residence of the Buddhist monks who immolated themselves in the 1960s to protest the war, and it houses the oldest school of music in the country. The magnificent Imperial Tombs that still survive here testify to the city's ancient splendor. The tombs are surrounded by large areas enclosed by walls, and each one has a courtyard, a pavilion, and a terrace. The most majestic of all the Imperial Tombs is the tomb of Minh Mang, built by his successor on the left bank of the Perfumed River between 1841 and 1843. Hue also has pagodas, temples, churches, and the strange Notre Dame Cathedral, which is modern but incorporates elements of traditional Vietnamese architecture.

Hue was devastated by one of the bloodiest battles of the war, but it has been partially restored. The halls of the Forbidden City (the residence of the emperor and his concubines) have been restored, and thousands of hours of work have restored the Ming chinoiserie that decorates the 60 buildings of the City of Purple and the Sun and Moon Gates. The restoration has brought new life to the Imperial Citadel's 148 acres of splendor, which celebrate the gentleness of bygone days and the elegance of a vanished civilization.

Tourists can visit the Temple of the Generations, the Valley of Tombs, the Palace of Supreme Harmony, and the Library, enveloped in lotus flowers and wild ginseng and set in a landscape of pastel shades that stretches as far as the sloping banks of the Perfumed River. Today, a music school for young students is housed in a side pavilion, and the school evokes the orchestras of lithophones and other percussion instruments that accompanied official ceremonies. The citadel has regained its thousand-year-old peace.

89 center
The interior of the temple dedicated to the cult of the dynasty of the Nguyen emperors at Hue.

89 bottom
Animal sculptures protect the entry to the mausoleum of Minh Mang, fourth son of Gia Long and second king of the Nguyen dynasty. The mausoleum was built between 1841 and 1843.

90 top
This banquet pavilion is in the Forbidden Purple City, which along with the Yellow Wall stands within Kinh Tanh, the enclosure erected by Gia Long.

90 bottom
The Thai Hoa Palace, or Supreme Harmony Palace, built in 1805 by Gia Long and restored for the last time by Khai Dinh in 1924, is the most important building in the Imperial City of Hue. Used for receptions and ceremonies, it is one of the few palaces that is still in excellent condition.

91–94 The interior of the Mieu Temple is well preserved. The temple is dedicated to the sovereigns of the Nguyen dynasty and holds the relics of seven Nguyen emperors, plus steles of the three revolutionary emperors, added in 1959.

95 top
In front of Hiem Lam Nac, or the Pavilion of Splendor, one of the very few buildings of the Imperial City still intact, are nine urns, each of which weighs up to 5,500 pounds and represents an emperor in the Nguyen dynasty.

95 bottom
Ngo Mon, the Midday Gate, built in 1834 by Minh Mang, is overlooked by Lau Ngu Phung, the Belvedere of the Five Phoenixes, which was used for formal ceremonies.

THE TRIUMPH OF A LUXURIANT VEGETATION

THE NORTH

96 top right
A round basket waterproofed with pitch is a typical means of transportation on the water. Baskets are also used for fishing and moving from one boat to another. This photo was taken in the village of Van Lam, near Hanoi, an area full of rice paddies. Rice has always been a staple of the Vietnamese diet.

The countryside north of Hue resembles a classic Chinese pen and ink drawing, all swollen clouds and dragon's-tooth pinnacles, with forests that invade the Central Highlands and slope down to the bright green rice fields called *dat nuoc* (earth and water, although the term is also synonymous with homeland) that stretch as far as the Red River Delta. This is the legendary Tonkin. It is also the former North Vietnam, a region that was and still

96 left
A peasant working in a northern rice paddy. Thanks to available water and the favorable climate, the Vietnamese have been able to transform the northern plains into an immense, brilliant green rice paddy.

is very poor and at least five years behind the south. There are few places of interest along the north-central coast apart from the village of Kim Lien, where Ho Chi Minh was born in 1890. The house where he was born is preserved as a sanctuary.

96 bottom right
Much of the hard work in the rice paddies is done with the help of water buffaloes.

97 *In the northern part of the country you can use a basket to fish in the rice paddies.*

98 top left
Visitors to the Perfumed Pagoda can take boat trips, go for walks, and explore the caves.

98 top right
Bicycles can be loaded with an enormous amount of material.

98 bottom left
The Long Bien Bridge, which was once called Doumer, after the name of its architect, is the oldest bridge leading into the city of Hanoi. Dating back to 1902, it is now reserved to trains, cyclists and pedestrians.

98 bottom right
Boats leave from the pier on the Perfumed River for a visit to the Perfumed Pagoda, where souls are purified, pain is relieved, and treatments for infertility are dispensed.

98–99 *The Perfumed Pagoda and the other pagodas in the area,*

built in the cavities of the calcareous rock, are visited by throngs of the faithful during a festival that takes place during the months of March and April. The photograph shows the pier with boats waiting to carry believers to the caves.

100–101 *A number of boats slide along the tranquil waters of the Perfumed River, traveling toward Chua Huong (the Perfumed Pagoda), a complex of pagodas and Buddhist sanctuaries about 37 miles southwest of Hanoi.*

102 top
The old Presidential Palace, the residence of the former governor of Hanoi, is an elegant, colonial-style building on Hung Vuong Street, near the Mausoleum of Ho Chi Minh.

102–103 *The Hanoi Opera Theater, along with the cathedral, various hotels, and many colonial villas, is part of Hanoi's architectural heritage.*
The legation quarter was largely untouched by the war but is now threatened by urban redevelopment.

HANOI

103 top
In Hanoi, any usable means of transportation will do in a pinch, like this sidecar.

103 center
An example of the villas built by the French in the residential area of Hanoi during the colonial period.

103 bottom
A group of women, the traditional carrying poles on their shoulders, passes the old Presidential Palace on their way to the market.

Hanoi's French buildings, constructed in 1920s or in turn-of-the-century style, remained undamaged after the war but now face the onslaught of speculators. New economic reforms are bringing prosperity to Hanoi, but the seat of power is also riddled with widespread corruption. Hanoi is a beautiful city, with an understated elegance and almost Nordic severity, and it has a delightful lake in the center of the city.

The air in Hanoi is full of the melodious, nasal songs broadcast by the loudspeakers of the pavement cafés. There are no cars, but a throng of bicycles in the streets. Designed by the French on a grandiose scale to resemble Paris, bombed by the Americans, never appreciated by the Russians, and considered no more than a bunker by the communist rulers, Hanoi is still one of the most fascinating cities in Asia. It is sober, austere, and still poor, with the 19th-century charm and petit bourgeois gentleness that the French always gave their colonies. Hanoi is a place to escape from the present with the certain expectation of a better future.

The biggest problem Hanoi faces today is how to save itself from modernization and avoid turning into another Bangkok, Taipei, or Seoul. Although it was largely untouched by the bombing of the war and the Asian boom of the 1980s, the city will not easily escape modernization, despite restoration projects. The famous Hoa Lo Prison, known as the Hanoi Hilton to the American soldiers incarcerated there, has been demolished to make way for a 22-story hotel. The site was supposed to have become a museum.

Disquieting signs of the worst kind of consumerism have appeared on the crumbling walls and in some shops. But Hanoi still shows many signs of poverty and of the spartan, pitiless life the city's residents endured during and after the war. As a result, it is commonly said that the Hanoi regime won the war but lost the peace. Now that renovation has begun in Hanoi, and the Vietnamese are once again receptive to Western language, music, films, and clothes, many believe that the United States lost the war but won the peace.

The face of the city changes from day to day: Buddhist temples are being restored, artists are painting abstracts, and teenagers play heavy metal music. The one thing that remains untouched is the Ho Chi Minh Mausoleum, a replica of Lenin's, which stands in the center of a square next to the Presidential Palace. The tomb where his successors buried him (despite his request for his body to be cremated

107 top left
The French architects who worked in Vietnam sometimes had little respect for the local culture. St. Joseph Cathedral is a clear example of disrespectful building practices: The Bao Tien Pagoda was torn down to make way for the church.

107 top right
The Quan Su Pagoda is one of the numerous so-called minor buildings in Hanoi.

the sacrifice of the two Trung sisters, heroines of the campaign against Chinese invaders in the first century AD. The building known as the Ambassadors' Pagoda, where envoys from Buddhist countries were accommodated, has become a religious center. Hanoi has numerous museums—the History, Army, Revolution, Independence, Air Force, and Fine Arts Museums—of revolutionary inspiration, including the Ho Chi Minh Museum next to the mausoleum. The museum displays extraordinary propaganda posters. The city's Catholic cathedral is neo-Gothic in style.

Dozens of cheap lodging houses have opened in Hanoi in the past few years. An excellent luxury hotel is the Metropol Pullman Sofitel, just a stone's throw from the lake and built in 1911 in an elegant colonial style. Many tourists prefer to stay at the Military Guest House, especially if they can reserve the suite where Henry Kissinger often stayed.

Dictatorship is dead and buried in the north, and democracy has arrived, following the example of China, Taiwan, the Koreas, and all the Asian countries that endured despotic regimes that believed they could have development without growth, a free market without a free press, and perestroika without glasnost. These regimes have been undermined by young people who insist on affirming their convictions,

108 top
Music is played and poetry recited within the Pavilion of the Pleiades, in the third courtyard of the Temple of Literature. Small orchestras often play here, using various traditional Vietnamese instruments.

108 bottom
This photograph shows the interior of a temple crowded with the faithful, with their hands joined in the typical act of prayer and numerous votive offerings carefully lined up on the altar.

109 top left
The enchanting, rich interior of the Ba Da Pagoda, which is located in an alleyway in front of the cathedral.

109 top right
Religious objects in the Ba Da Pagoda.

110 top left
This shop on a street in the historic downtown area of Hanoi sells red and yellow communist flags. The star and hammer and sickle motifs, yellow on a red background, are among the most popular for T-shirts.

110 bottom left
A view of Hang Bac, or Jewelry Street. All the streets in the old city center have kept their original names, which indicated the trades that could be found there.

clandestine satellite TV aerials, Catholics demonstrating against past persecution, dissident Vietnamese, and émigrés who send home $3 billion a year in foreign currency and hold considerable political power.

Today, Hanoi is a city devoted to business and trade. Every street in the city is a market. All it takes to set yourself up in business is somewhere to sit down; you need only to hang a mirror from the branch of a tree to open a barbershop. Thousands of people come in from the countryside to sell their produce on the pavements every day. Near the lake is the famous Hang Gai Street, in the old quarter that occupies the area bounded by Hoan Kiem Lake, the Citadel, Dong Xuan Market, and the ramparts of the Red River, where every street is devoted to a different trade and named after the products on sale: Silk Street, Paper Street, Lantern Street, Toy Street, Bamboo Street, Medicine Street, Rice Street, Grilled Fish Street, Noodle Street, and Jewelry Street.

Shops and restaurants, together with hotels, were the first to benefit from economic liberalization. Today, shopping in Hanoi no longer means visiting a huge government department store with empty shelves. Hanoi's streets are once again full of color and life, many buildings have been renovated, and joint ventures are a fact of life,

110 top right
Little open-air restaurants are common in Hanoi, like this one on a street in the French quarter. All you need is a cooking stove, the necessary ingredients, and perhaps a chair to accommodate the occasional customer to open up a small business that is bound to grow.

110 bottom right
To Westerners, traditional Chinese masks are amusing and not frightening as they are to Orientals, to whom they represent spirits and deities that are often evil and must be exorcised to avoid bad luck and illness.

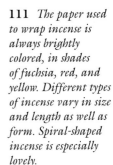

111 *The paper used to wrap incense is always brightly colored, in shades of fuchsia, red, and yellow. Different types of incense vary in size and length as well as form. Spiral-shaped incense is especially lovely.*

112–113 *Boats with dragon-wing sails ply the waters of Ha Long Bay. The name Ha Long means Dragon Descending, in memory of an ancient legend that tells of the descent of a dragon into the bay. The zone is becoming a major tourist area, despite a certain risk of pollution from mineral mining.*

112 top
Ha Long Bay is considered the eighth wonder of the world, as well as the most beautiful place in Vietnam. Many films have been shot here, and the area's reputation continues to grow. You can rent boats and take lovely cruises amid thousands of islands, some no larger than a boulder tossed into the sea. The area has a number of colonial-era hotels that offer old-fashioned luxuries: large rooms, blade fans, and four-poster beds.

especially in the hotel trade. And the exporting industries of Hanoi and the entire north have enormous economic potential for additional growth.

French tourists often visit Hanoi, which is still associated with Vietnam's long colonial history, and all of them go to see the Dien Bien Phu Battlefield, which is still covered with wreckage, where cavalry Colonel Christian de Castries led 25,000 colonial paratroops and legionnaires to the greatest military defeat in French history. Other places of interest around Hanoi include pagodas scattered over a hilly landscape of rare beauty; the mountain resort of Tam Dao (which the French called Cascade d'Argent), with colonial villas and resembling unspoiled Dalat before the advent of tourism; and Hoa Lu, the ancient capital before the year 1000, with sanctuaries and grottos only equalled in beauty by Ha Long Bay, which features one of the loveliest landscapes in the country. Ha Long Bay, which is 99 miles east of Hanoi, contains thousands of islands—a very large one, a few medium-sized, and numerous oddly shaped small ones—in a deep blue sea. Only three are inhabited, the largest being Cat Ba. Pearl oysters are cultivated at Quang Lan, and there is fresh water on another, teapot-shaped island. You can cruise around the islands, perhaps to see the pelican cave where three stone Buddhas appear to be

113 top
A group of fishermen waits for boats in the port of Hongai. In the background, islands emerge from the deep blue water.

113 center
Fishermen pull their nets to shore, hoping to find them full of choice shrimp from Ha Long Bay.

113 bottom
A traditional fishing boat glides slowly on the waters of Ha Long Bay.

114 *Northern Vietnam, near Sapa in the province of Hoang Lien Son, which borders China to the north, has extraordinary natural landscapes. This area is still inhabited by a Hmong minority of Meo extraction.*

playing chess, or pass between two islands so close together that the passage is called the Gateway to Paradise. A good hotel is Ha Long No. 1, where Catherine Deneuve stayed while she was filming *Indochina*. There are also many restaurants along the seafront.

Haiphong, the third most populous city in Vietnam, the largest industrial city in the north, and one of the major ports, offers no particular attractions. Places of

114–115 *A placid river bordered by rice paddies, with gentle hills in the background, provides a typical landscape in the Hoa Lu area south of Hanoi.*

interest nearby include Do Son Beach, a favorite with the expatriate community living in Hanoi, and Cat Ba National Park.

115 top
The mountainous countryside at the Chinese border is particularly verdant, very rainy, and cold during winter. But the mountains, which are quite high, have never been an insurmountable obstacle for foreign invaders during the long centuries of the country's troubled history.

Vietnam was a meeting point for the great Asian and Oceanic migrations, and the country's primary ethnic races are Indonesian and Mongoloid, Melanesian, Negrito, and Australoid. Almost 90% of the population of more than 70 million are Vietnamese. Around 2% are Chinese, who mostly live in the south, in the Cholon district of Ho Chi Minh City. A shopper's paradise, Cholon, with its slums and red pagodas shrouded in a mist of incense, was recently featured in Annaud's film *The Lover*. The rest of Vietnam's population are ethnic minorities, mainly Khmer and Cham, together with 60 different ethnolinguistic groups. Some ruined monuments, such as the tower-shaped brick sanctuaries, are the work of the Chams, whose civilization was suppressed by the neighboring populations. Vietnam also has mountain-dwelling populations (called Montagnards by the French), who live in the Central Highlands and the mountainous regions of the north. The Montagnards can be divided into three main linguistic groups and have not wholly adopted the customs of the Vietnamese majority.

The original Vietnamese religion, polytheism or animism, is still close to the hearts of the population, together with ancestor worship. When the Chinese invaded Vietnam, they brought with them

116 top left
An elderly Vietnamese from Tay Ninh sports a white goatee.

116 bottom left
A war veteran, now retired, wears his uniform and the decorations he received.

116 top right
Two girls from Ho Chi Minh City, with loose hair and European clothes, smile for the photographer.

116 bottom right
The Vietnamese are good-natured and smile often, like this young man.

117 *A straw hat decorated with flowers frames the pretty face of a young Vietnamese. In the north, the people are more reserved than in the south, perhaps because they are not as accustomed to contact with the Western world, but it is not difficult to make direct contact. The people do not mind questions about their age, families, and income, and these subjects can be a good way to start a conversation. Moreover, although the Vietnamese are often shy, they are quite curious and can scarcely wait for a chance to speak what little they know of a foreign language and strike up a new friendship.*

118 *This young woman with a conical hat was photographed in her small grocery store.*

Confucianism, the official doctrine of the imperial civil service examinations from 1706 to 1919. Confucianism was adopted by all the Vietnamese imperial dynasties. Today, Buddhism is represented by the Thyen Mahayana School, which coexists with the Hinayana or Theravada School. Vietnam's third religion is Taoism. The attitude of governments and people to Christianity, which was introduced by Western missionaries on several occasions, has varied over the years from acceptance to prohibition and persecution. Today, the Vietnamese Catholic Church has at least 5 million worshippers. Islam and Hinduism are also represented in the country. Most Vietnamese consider themselves Buddhists, but they actually follow Confucianism in their daily practices and Taoism in their interpretation of the world.

In practice, the three religions are officially combined in Caodaism, a religion founded in 1919 by Ngo Van Chieu, a civil servant in the French administration. Ngo Van Chieu's Caodaism incorporates aspects of Christianity, Islam, ancestor worship, and sky worship and venerates famous saints from all over the world, including among their ranks historical and literary personalities such as Napoléon, Joan of Arc, Victor Hugo, and Louis Pasteur. The Holy See of the Caodaist religion is in the village of

119 top left
Many areas of Vietnam are rainy, and raincoats have to be very wide to fit over a bicycle.

119 bottom left
A man selling colored balloons walks through the market on Ho Chi Minh City's Yersin Street, one of the many smaller, yet always crowded markets of the city.

119 top right
A couple rushes by on a motorcycle on their way to a wedding ceremony.

119 bottom right
This girl, a student photographed on a Da Nang Street, is wearing the traditional girl's uniform known as ao dai. The national costume for Vietnamese women is a knee-length jacket, with a Korean collar and two slits along the sides, worn over a pair of wide pants.

Long Than in Tay Ninh (Tanyin) Province, some 62 miles west of Ho Chi Minh City. The cathedral-pagoda was built in 1927 in a Chinese-exotic-eclectic style, with dragons coiling around the pillars and statues of every divinity and prophet in the world, including Jesus, Confucius, Buddha, Brahma, Shiva, and Vishnu. In his book *The Quiet American*, Graham Greene described it as "a Walt Disney fantasia of the East." The symbol of Caodaism is a huge eye surrounded by rays, and the priest-cum-mediums act as intermediaries between God and the congregation. Caodaism was repressed by the French from 1937 to 1946; today, the religion has about 2 million followers.

Caodaism is remarkable, but other unusual religions have emerged from the Mekong Delta, one of the last Asian frontiers remaining to be explored by tourists, with more than 2 million acres of canals and mangrove swamps. The lesser-known Hoa Hao, for instance, preaches a return to purity and simplicity through meditation and fasting. The sect, which has had a turbulent history like Caodaism, evolving from revelation to evangelism and from politics to armed warfare, now has more than a million followers.

120 top left
This little girl belongs to the Montagnard ethnic group, who live in the Central Highlands on the Laotian border.

120 bottom left
The photo shows the unique clothing of a girl in the Black Tribe ethnic group, in the region bordering China.

120 top right
Hmong ethnic groups live near the Chinese border.

120 bottom right
Members of the An Don group, from the Central Highlands.

121 *This young Hmong woman from the Sapa region in the northern part of the country has almond eyes like the Chinese and is wearing large hoop earrings and an outfit of handmade cloth dyed in a special, very deep indigo color.*

122–123 *These young girls at work in the fields are members of the Hmong ethnic group, in the Mong Cai area in northern Vietnam.*

122 top left
Women workers dress in white in the northern coal mines of Cam Pha.

122 top right
This young girl from Son La is a member of the Meo ethnic group.

123 top left
This woman from the Zao ethnic group in the Sapa region wears a large red turban and silver earrings.

123 top right
This beautiful costume belongs to an ethnic group that lives in Lang Son in northern Vietnam.

123 bottom left
A member of a Thai minority near Son La proudly shows off his traditional costume.

125 *The perfumed smoke of the incense offered by this girl rises to the gods in the Thien Hau Temple in the Cholon quarter of Ho Chi Minh City. The Temple of Thien Hau, or the Celestial Lady, is dedicated to the goddess who protects sailors and is visited primarily by women. The offerings of votive paper are burned in an oven to the right of the altar.*

124 top left
A procession of Buddhist monks, with their extraordinary yellow parasols, passes through the streets of Hue. These monks are from the same sect that publicly immolated themselves to protest the corrupt South Vietnamese regime.

124 bottom left
This procession of monks was photographed in northern Vietnam, with a characteristic temple in the background. The temple has pagoda-shaped roofs, a clear sign of Chinese architectural influence.

124 top right
This old monk rests at the door to the Perfumed Temple in Hanoi.

124 bottom right
The interior of the Khue Van Pavilion, in the third courtyard of the Temple of Literature in Hanoi.

Of the many festivals celebrated in Vietnam, the most important is Tet, a national festival that unites the whole country, from north to south, in preparations and celebrations. It falls between the winter solstice and the spring equinox, on the first day of the lunar year. The full name of the festival is Tet Nhuyen Dan (Festival of the First Morning of the Year). The Vietnamese are usually reserved, but Tet is an occasion when they let themselves go and have fun, like Carnival in the Latin countries. Above all, it is a time when the most ancient traditions and religious beliefs based on mythology, the concept of the family, and the universe and ancestor worship are evoked in a syncretism that has no equivalent in any other culture.

The Tet celebrations date back so far that there is no written documentation of their origin. The history of the celebrations during the imperial period is well known, however; under the Ly dynasty in the year 1000, regattas were held on the Red River, with imperial galleons, Buddhist rites, and banquets. Every dynasty introduced innovations into the official celebrations, such as theatrical performances and visits to ancestors, all of which were strictly observed by the emperors.

Tet does not last for a day, but for months. It starts on the twenty-third day of the twelfth month, a week before New Year's Eve, with a family ceremony in honor of the household gods. This is a rite of propitiation, because the household gods, who have burned their trousers by standing too close to the fire, ascend to heaven to present their report, which will hopefully be a benevolent one. In their absence, an emblem of Buddha called a *khan* (an earthenware slab and a yellow cloth fixed to a pole) must be displayed

in the home to ward off the evil spirits always lurking close by. In towns, TV aerials serve the purpose very well. When offerings have been made to the household gods and the most terrifying demons kept at bay, the family can relax and turn to decorating their home and preparing food, especially rice cakes.

Evil spirits are an obsession with the Vietnamese, who try to protect themselves in every possible way, with branches of peach or apricot blossom, fireworks, and lanterns. The celebrations create the right atmosphere for the return to earth of the spirits of the ancestors, who are worshipped on the first day of Tet. Everything good or bad, beautiful or ugly that happens on the first day of

the year foretells what will happen for the rest of the year.

Members of the family exchange gifts of money wrapped in red paper; draw up horoscopes based on the Chinese tradition of animals; plan walks in search of their kindred spirit; and write poetry and maxims to be displayed in the center of the home. On the third day, the spirits of the ancestors, now satisfied, go back to heaven; the fourth day is a working day; and on the seventh day, the household gods return from heaven, still without their trousers, so the emblems of Buddha are no longer needed. Thus ends what might be called the celebratory part of the

festival, involving offerings of flowers and food, and the fairs and parties begin. The second part of the festival, which is pure entertainment, lasts until the beginning of summer.

To fully appreciate Vietnamese culture, the first thing Western visitors must do is to forget their criteria of beauty. In Vietnamese architecture, for example, the starting point for the construction of all buildings, from the birthplace to the tomb, from temples to imperial palaces, is geomantic. Geomancy is the art of achieving harmony with nature by observation of the stars and the use of special instruments. Only in this way can harmoniously oriented, formed, and connected buildings be erected. To a Western visitor's eye, Vietnamese buildings, whether they are pagodas or ordinary houses, are mysteriously charming.

The oldest traces of indigenous architecture in Vietnam are found in the ancient capital, Co Loa, which has

126 left
The warm atmosphere of the Quan Su Pagoda in Hanoi, where the worshippers pray among golden friezes.

126 right
A detail of the Tran Vu Temple in Hanoi. Votive offers are represented by different types of flowers.

127 left
The interior of the Tran Vu Temple in Hanoi. Although small, the temple is richly decorated. The offerings of the faithful are placed on the altar in front of the statue of the god.

127 top right
The single-pillared Chua Mot Cot Pagoda in Hanoi, built in 1049 during the Ly dynasty.

127 bottom right
Monks wearing traditional colorful clothing follow the funeral procession of a bonze in a Hanoi street.

ruins dating from the 2nd century AD and is still visible on the outskirts of Hanoi. Vietnamese architecture was strongly influenced by the Chinese during their long period of domination, but Vietnamese architects gradually broke away and found their own identity from the 16th to the end of the 18th century. A magnificent example of Vietnamese architecture is the fortified city of Hue, the impressive capital of Vietnam when it was united under the Nguyen dynasty. When it was designed, Emperor Gia Long was inspired by the buildings of Beijing, and he drew on the works of Vauban for the fortifications. The Citadel is bounded to the south by the Perfumed River, and the three other sides are protected by moats. The city has three concentric sections with a square plan, with fortresses, inner enclosures, and the Forbidden Purple Enclosure, which contains the emperor's private residence. Nothing in the building of the Citadel was left

to chance; its design follows geomantic concepts that take account of the contrasting forces of good and evil that move heaven and earth and govern the destiny of man.

Traditional sculpture in Vietnam depicted religious figures; statues made of stone or decorated or lacquered wood are to be found in the temples and pagodas. Villages have communal buildings devoted to social functions and sometimes

128 top left
The cathedral of the Cao Dai religion is in the Tay Ninh region in the south. Caodaism, created in 1919 by Ngo Van Chieu, is an attempt to join all existing faiths in Vietnam under a single supreme creator.

serving as places to display local crafts. The north is seeing a revival of the art of wood carving, which was lost during the French domination. Especially in Bach Ninh Province, entire families make colored prints showing the same human and animal characters, always belonging to country life, with the same sense of humor as the extraordinary water-puppet shows.

Performances of Vietnamese water-puppet shows are exhilarating, with dragons playing ball, exquisite dances, amusing gags about darting fish and incapable fishermen, folk dances, and children's games. The stage of the Water Puppet Show is the surface of a great tank of water, and

the puppeteers, hidden behind a curtain and immersed in water up to their waists, move the puppets with long bamboo poles. The shows are usually preceded by concerts of traditional music.

Music, like dancing, has an ancient tradition in Vietnam. It has obviously been strongly influenced by the music of China and the Hindu Champa kingdom. Vietnamese music probably developed gradually, but it is believed to date from between 1428 and 1788, when the emperors of the Le dynasty commissioned a series of works to be performed on court, social, and religious occasions. The emperors were also responsible for organizing the orchestras.

128 bottom left
The richness and extravagance of the Caodaist temple's decorations.

128 top right
The exterior of the cathedral. The photograph shows a row of windows along the side walls of the temple.

128 bottom right
Seated in prayer, the faithful wear brightly colored tunics.

128–129
Spectacular ceremonies often take place inside the cathedral, attracting many tourists.

130–131 *This traditional, lavishly decorated pirogue was photographed during a race on the Saigon River. All rowers wear brilliantly colored costumes.*

130 top left
A scene from a traditional Vietnamese drama presented in the Thu Do Theater in the Chinese quarter in Ho Chi Minh City.

130 top right
Ho Chi Minh City's Chinese quarter has numerous little temples and brightly colored dragons. The photo shows a dragon-shaped boat.

131 top
During the Tet Festival, which is the Chinese New Year, the Dragon Dance is performed along the streets of the Chinese quarter of Ho Chi Minh City.

131 bottom
A young girl in an extraordinary full-dress costume, complete with little crossed flags on her back.

Folk music is also a part of Vietnam's musical heritage. All minorities and regions of the country have a rich local musical tradition, with Chinese influences in the north and Champa influences of Indian origin in the south. The music of the coastal provinces invokes the spirits of the sea, the songs of the country districts tell of work in the fields, and love songs are sung everywhere.

A special type of chamber music is performed by small orchestras with the participation of female voices, but only in the largest towns, to entertain a few intellectuals gathered for the occasion. It consists of sung poems narrating important episodes in Vietnamese history. The singers are accompanied by lithophones and lutes. Finally, Buddhist music also has an important place on the country's musical scene; it may be orchestrated or performed with musical tones by reciting voices accompanied by drums.

The arts might be said to include fortune-telling; the Vietnamese zodiac is similar to the Chinese version and is based on the year of birth. Every year in the lunar calendar has a sign, and there are 12 signs, which are repeated every 12 years—the mouse, ox, tiger, rabbit, dragon, snake, horse, goat, monkey, cock, dog, and pig. The year 2000 will be the year of the dragon.

INDEX

c = caption

A

Acupuncture, 105
Advertising, 57c
Air Force Museum, 108
Ambassadors' Pagoda, 108
Amerasians, 29c
Amusement parks, 73
Ancestor worship, 116, 124
An Don people, 120c
Animism, 116
Annam, 8, 24c
Annaud, Jean-Jacques, 116
Ao dai uniform, 55c, 119c
Appelius, Mario, 30c
Architecture, 126–127
Army Museum, 108

B

Bac Bo, 8
Bach Dang River, Battle of the, 22, 23c
Bach Ma Mountain, 75c
Bach Ninh Province, 128
Ba Da Pagoda, 109c
Bai Non Nuoc (China Beach), 8c, 86
Ba Na, 86, 89
Bao Dai, Emperor, 36, 37c, 39, 40c, 88c
Baskets, 71c, 96c
Beaches, 8c, 75, 75c, 86, 114
Ben Nghe Restaurant, 58c
Bhadravaman, King, 77c
Bicycles, 98c
Bigeard, Col., 39c
Bin Dinh Province, 2c, 83c
Binh Soup Shop, 64
Binh Tay Market, 58c
Black Flag army, 32c, 34c
Black Goddess Mountain, 68
Black Tribe ethnic group, 120c
Botanical and Zoological Gardens (Ho Chi Minh City), 64c
Bridges, 79c, 98c, 108c
Buddha statues, 64c, 65c, 66c
Buddhism, 23, 66c, 119
Buddhist monks, 124c, 127c
  immolations by, 43, 43c
Buon Me Thuot, 81c

C

Cai Rang, 68c
Cambodia, 8, 26, 41c
  U.S. bombing of, 46
  Vietnamese intervention, 51
Cam Rahn Bay, 75
Caodaism, 119–120, 127c, 128c
Castries, Col. Christian de, 113
Cat Ba Island, 113
Cat Ba National Park, 11, 114
Catechism, Vietnamese, 26c
Cave of the Buddha, 84c
Caverns, 73, 84c
Central Highlands, 11, 68, 70
Cha Ban, 75
Cham art, 12c, 20c
Cham Museum, 12c
Champa kingdom, 20, 20c, 21c, 66c, 89
Cham people, 67c, 75, 116
China, 8, 39
  rule over Vietnam, 20, 22
China Beach, 8c, 86
Chinese Han invaders, 22c
Chinese influence in Vietnam, 67c
Cholon quarter. *See under* Ho Chi Minh City
Cho Quan Church, 61
Christianity, 26c, 66c, 77, 119
Chua Mot Cot Pagoda, 105, 127c
Chua Phuk Kien Pagoda, 79c
Churches
  Hanoi, 107c, 108
  Ho Chi Minh City, 61, 64
  Hue, 89
Church of Cha Tam, 64
Citadel. *See* Forbidden City
City Hall (Ho Chi Minh City), 64c
City of Purple, 89
Climate, 8, 11
Cloud Hill, 75c, 86
Coal mines, 122c
Cochin China, 8
Cogny, Col. René, 39c
Co Loa, 126–127
Communal buildings, 127–128
Communist rule in Vietnam, 50–52, 53c
Con Dao Archipelago, 68
Confucianism, 23, 66c, 116, 119
Confucius, 67c
Costumes of southern Indochina, 28c
Cu Chi, 68, 71c
Cuc Phuong National Park, 11

D

Dalat, 11, 70, 73, 73c
Da Nang, 8c, 12c, 81c, 83c, 86
Da Nang Museum, 83c
Dance, 128
De Giapon, Gen., 45c
Democratic Republic of Vietnam, 39
Deneuve, Catherine, 114
Dien Bien Phu, Battle of, 39, 40c, 41c, 42c
Dien Bien Phu Battlefield, 113
Dien Huu Pagoda, 105
Dong So culture, 20
Do Son Beach, 114
Dragon Dance, 131c
Dragons, 2c, 8
Dragon-wing boats, 112c
Drums, 20c
Dupuis, Jean, 34c

E

Ecole Française d'Extrême Orient, 86
Ethnic groups, 29c, 68, 70, 116, 120c, 122c, 123c
Executions, 36c, 48c

F

Facial features of Vietnamese people, 11c
Fauna, 11
Festivals, 61c, 124, 126, 131c
Fine Arts Museum, 108
Fishermen, 68c, 70c, 75c, 113c
Floating Hotel, 56, 56c
Floating markets, 68c
Flower arrangement, 55c
Forbidden City, 89, 90c, 127
Forest in the House, 73
Forests, 11
Fortune-telling, 131
French colonialism, 8, 32, 36, 39, 42, 113
  conquest of Vietnam, 32c, 34c, 35c
  first contacts, 23c
  French rule, 36c, 37c
  war for independence, 39c, 40c, 41c, 42c
Funan kingdom, 20

G

Gajasimba (elephant-lion), 83c
Gardener's Cottage, 105
Garnier, Francis, 34c
Gate of Humanity, 2c
Gateway to Paradise, 114
General Post Office building (Ho Chi
   Minh City), 55, 56c
Geneva Accords, 41c, 42
Geography of Vietnam, 8
Geomancy, 126
Giac Lam Pagoda, 56, 61
Giac Vien Pagoda, 61
Gia Long, Emperor, 26, 90c, 127
Gian, 89
Goldwater, Barry, 44
Gougah Caves, 73
Grand-Hotel de la Rotonde, 37c
Greene, Graham, 58c, 120
Gulf of Tongking Resolution, 44, 44c

H

Haiphong, 39, 40c, 47, 114
Ha Long Bay, 112c, 113–114, 113c
Ha Long No. 1 (hotel), 114
Hanoi, 23
   business and trade, 110, 110c, 113
   churches, 107c, 108
   climate, 11
   French buildings, 103, 103c
   French conquest of, 34c
   Hang Bac Street, 110c
   Hang Gai Street, 110
   Ho Chi Minh sites, 103, 105, 105c
   Ho Hoan Kiem Lake, 106, 106c
   hotels, 105c, 108
   legation quarter, 102c
   modernization threat, 103
   museums, 105c, 108
   pagodas, 105, 106, 106c, 107c, 108,
      108c, 109c, 126c, 127c
   restaurants, 110c
   in 17th century, 25c
   streets and districts, 25c
   temples, 106, 108c, 126c, 127c
   traffic, 105c
   Vietnam War destruction, 47, 50c
Hanoi Hilton (prison), 103
Hanoi Opera Theater, 102c
Hiem Lam Nac, 95c
Highway 1, 84c
Hinduism, 66c, 119
Hindu statues, 12c, 66c, 83c

Historical buildings (Hoi An), 77
History Museum, 108
Hmong people, 114c, 120c, 122c
Hoa Hao sect, 120
Hoa Lo Prison, 103
Hoa Lu, 8c, 9c, 113, 114c
Hoang Lien Son Province, 114c
Ho Chi Minh, 36, 38-39, 40c, 42c,
   43c, 45c
   birthplace, 96
   Hanoi residence, 105
   life history, 38c
   mausoleum, 103, 105, 105c
   museum about, 64, 64c, 108
Ho Chi Minh Archaeological Museum,
   105c
Ho Chi Minh City (Saigon)
   boat rides, 58c
   changes since 1975, 30c
   Cholon quarter, 2c, 31c, 56, 57c,
      58c, 61c, 64, 67, 116, 124c, 131c
   churches, 61, 64
   City Hall, 64c
   climate, 11
   Dong Khoi Street, 55
   economic importance, 30c
   fall to Communist forces, 52c, 53c
   French conquest of, 35c
   hotels, 55–56, 56c, 58c
   markets, 31c, 58c, 67, 119c
   mosques, 61, 64
   museums, 64, 64c
   nightlife, 58c
   pagodas, 2c, 56, 61, 61c, 64
   port area, 55c
   restaurants, 58c
   rivers and canals, 31c, 55c, 58c
   temples, 61, 124c
   traffic, 55, 55c
   Yersin Street, 58c
   zoo, 64c
Ho Chi Minh Museum, 64, 64c, 108
Ho Chi Minh Trail, 89
Ho Hoan Kiem Lake, 106, 106c
Hoi An, 75, 77, 78c, 79c
Hon Chong Peninsula, 70c
Hongai, 113c
Hong-Hoa, Battle of, 32c
Hotel Continental, 56, 58c
Hotels
   Ha Long Bay, 113c, 114
   Hanoi, 105c, 108
   Ho Chi Minh City, 55–56, 56c, 58c
House of a Hundred Roofs, 73
Hue, 9c, 26, 86, 86c, 89

architecture, 127
Forbidden City (Citadel), 89, 90c,
   127
gates, 2c, 89, 95c
pagodas, 12c
temples, 89c, 90c
tombs, 12c, 86c, 88c, 89, 89c
Vietnam War, 50c, 51c
Hugo, Victor, 119

I

Immolations by Buddhist monks, 43,
   43c
Imperial Tombs, 89
Incense, 110c
Independence Museum, 108
Independence period (939–1858),
   22–23, 26
Indochina (film), 114
Indochinese Communist Party, 38, 38c
International Control Commission,
   43c
Islam, 119

J

Jade Emperor Pagoda, 61
Jade Mountain Temple, 106, 108c
Japanese occupation of Indochina, 38,
   38c
Joan of Arc, 119
Johnson, Lyndon B., 44, 44c, 46
Junks, 58c

K

Kennedy, John F., 44c
Kent State shootings, 46
Khai Dinh, Emperor, 36, 37c, 90c
   mausoleum of, 12c, 88c
Khan (Buddha emblem), 124
Khmer Krom people, 68c
Khmer people, 20
Khmer Rouge, 51
Khue Van Pavilion, 124c
Kim Lien, 96
Kinh Tanh, 90c
Kissinger, Henry, 45c, 46, 108
Kublai Khan, 23, 23c

L

Lake of the Returned Sword, 106,
   106c

Lang Co Beach, 86
Lang Co Peninsula, 8c, 75c, 86, 89
Lang-Kep, Battle of, 32c
Lang Son, 123c
Laos, 8, 26, 41c
Lau Ngu Phung, 95c
Le Duc Tho, 45c, 46
Library, the (Hue), 89
Lien Khang Caves, 73
Long Bien Bridge, 98c
Long Than, 119–120
Lon Nol, Gen., 45c
Lover, The (film), 116
Ly dynasty, 23, 124, 128

M

Mailer, Norman, 49c
Maps
  Indochina, 14, 20c, 23c
  Tonkin and Annam, 24c
Marble Mountains, 84c, 86
Mariamman Temple, 61
Martin, Graham, 52c
Masks, 110c
McCarthy, Mary, 49c
Mekong Delta, 8, 68, 68c
Mekong River, 29c, 68
Meo people, 122c
Metropol Pullman Sofitel, 105c, 108
Michelin rubber plantation, 37c
Mieu Temple, 89c, 90c
Military Guest House, 108
Minh Mang Mausoleum, 86c, 89, 89c
Mongols, 22c
Monks. *See* Buddhist monks
Montagnards, 68, 116, 120c
Morse, Wayne, 45c
Mosques, 61, 64
Mountainous countryside at Chinese
  border, 115c
Museum of the Revolution, 64
Museums
  Da Nang, 12c, 83c, 86
  Hanoi, 105c, 108
  Ho Chi Minh City, 64, 64c
Music, 128, 131
My Lai, 75
My Son, 76c, 77c, 86, 89
Mythology of Vietnam, 8

N

Nam Bo, 8
Napoléon, 119

National College. *See* Temple of
  Literature
National History Museum, 64, 64c,
  65c, 67c
National parks, 11, 114
National Workers' Congress of
  Vietnam (1960), 43c
Na Trang, 11
Ngoc Son Temple, 106, 108c
Ngo Dinh Diem, 39c, 42–43, 64
Ngo dynasty, 22
Ngo Mon (Midday) Gate, 2c, 95c
Ngo Van Chieu, 119, 127c
Nguyen Anh, Emperor, 26
Nguyen Cahn, Prince, 26c
Nguyen dynasty, 22, 26
Nguyen Hoang, Emperor, 12c
Nguyen Khao Ky, Gen., 39c
Nguyen Ngoc Loan, 48c
Nguyen Van Thieu, Gen., 39c, 43
Nha Trang, 75, 75c, 81c
Nhu, Madame, 39c
Nixon, Richard, 44c, 45c, 46, 47
Notre Dame Cathedral (Ho Chi Minh
  City), 61
Notre Dame Cathedral (Hue), 89

O

Orchids, 29c

P

Pagodas
  Hanoi, 105, 106, 106c, 107c, 108,
    108c, 109c, 126c, 127c
  Ho Chi Minh City, 2c, 56, 61, 61c,
    64
  Hoi An, 79c
  Hue, 12c
  Perfumed Pagoda, 98c
Palace of Supreme Harmony, 89, 90c
Pasteur, Louis, 119
Pavilion of Splendor, 95c
Pavilion of the Pleiades, 106c, 108c
Peasant life, 11c
Pentagon Papers scandal, 46
Perfumed Pagoda, 98c
Perfumed River, 9c, 86c, 98c
Phan Tiet, 70c
Pigneau de Behaine, Pierre, 26, 26c
Pirogues, 28c, 130c
Plant species, 11
Po Klong Garai, 75, 76c
Po Nagar Temple, 76c, 77c

Pongour Caves, 73
Pren Caves, 73
Prenn, 73c
Presidential Palace (Hanoi), 102c,
  103c
Presidential Palace (Ho Chi Minh
  City), 52c, 64
Prisoners in French colonial period,
  36c
Prisons, 103
Prostitution, 75
Puppets, 58c, 128

Q

Quang Duc, Tich, 43, 43c
Quang Lan Island, 113
Quang Nam-Da Nang Province, 83c
Quan Su Pagoda, 107c, 126c
Quan Than Pagoda, 106
Quiet American, The (Greene), 58c,
  120
Qui Nhon, 2c, 75
Quoc-Ngu script, 26c, 77

R

Raincoats, 119c
Rashid al-Din, 22c
Red River Delta, 8
Reeducation camps, 70
Refugees from Vietnam, 47–48, 51,
  53c
Religions, 66c, 116, 119–120
Republic of South Vietnam, 42
Reserve of Vietnamese people, 116c
Restaurants
  Hanoi, 110c
  Ho Chi Minh City, 58c
Revolutionary League for the
  Independence of Vietnam.
  See Vietminh
Revolution Museum, 108
Rex Hotel, 55–56, 58c
Rhodes, Alexandre de, 24c, 26c, 77
Rice paddies, 9c, 15c, 96c
Rivière, Henri, 34c
Rubber plantations, 37c
Russell, Bertrand, 49c

S

Saigon. *See* Ho Chi Minh City
St. Joseph Cathedral, 107c
Sampans, 9c, 78c, 86c

Sculpture, 127
Sihanouk, Prince, 45c
Son La, 15c
Sontag, Susan, 49c
Son Tay, Battle of, 32c
South China Sea, 70c
South Vietnam National Liberation
   Front, 52c, 53c
Steles, 106, 106c
Straw hats, 11c, 68c, 119c
Student's uniform, 105c
Sun and Moon Gates, 89
Sun Ray Bridge, 108c
Surfing, 75c

T

Tam Dao, 113
Tam Giao (triple religion), 66c
Tam Son Hoi Quan Pagoda, 2c
Tan Son Nhat Airport, 52c
Taoism, 66c, 119
Tay Ninh Temple, 68
Temple of Literature (Van Mieu
   University), 23, 24c, 106, 106c,
   108c, 124c
Temple of the Generations, 89
Temple ruins, 8c
Temples
  Cu Chi, 68
  Hanoi, 106, 108c, 126c, 127c
  Ho Chi Minh City, 61, 124c
  Hue, 89c, 90c
  Po Nagar, 76c, 77c
Tet Festival, 61c, 124, 126, 131c
Tet Offensive (1968), 45
Thai minority, 123c
Theater, 131c
Thien Hau Pagoda, 61c
Thien Hau Temple, 124c
Thien Mu Pagoda, 12c
Thieu Tri, Emperor, 86c

Thong Nhat (Reunification)
   Conference Hall, 55c
Thu Bon River, 78c
Thu Do Theater, 131c
Tombs
  Hanoi, 103, 105, 105c
  Hue, 12c, 86c, 88c, 89, 89c
Tonkin, 8, 24c
Tonkin, royal palace of, 24c
Tran dynasty, 23
Trang Quoc Pagoda, 106, 106c
Tran Va Tra, Gen., 45c
Tran Vu Temple, 126c, 127c
Truch Bach Lake, 106
Trung Bo, 8
Trung sisters, 22c, 108
Tu Duc, Emperor, 32c
  mausoleum of, 88c, 89c
Turtle Pagoda, 106, 106c

U

Uma culture, 83c
United States, 39, 41c, 103. *See also*
   Vietnam War
  diplomatic relations with Vietnam, 52
U.S. former embassies, 56c, 64

V

Val, P. du, 23c
Valley of Love, 73
Valley of Tombs, 89
Van Lam, 96c
Van Mieu University. *See* Temple of
   Literature
Van Tieng Dung, Gen., 52c
Vatican Missionary-Ethnological
   Museum, 26c
Vegetable-drying, 11c
Vietcong, 43, 45, 45c
Vietminh, 38–39, 38c, 39c, 41c, 42c,

   43c
"Vietnam" name, origin of, 26
Vietnam War, 8c, 44–48, 44c, 45c,
   46c, 47c, 48c, 50, 50c, 51c, 52c, 86
  antiwar movement, 46, 49c
  fall of Saigon, 52c, 53c
  Gulf of Tongking Resolution, 44, 44c
  Hanoi, impact on, 47, 50c
  Hue, impact on, 50c, 51c
  museum about, 64
  peace talks, 45c, 46
  Tet Offensive (1968), 45
Vinh Nghiem Pagoda, 61c
Vo Nguyen Giap, Gen., 39, 41c
Vung Tau Peninsula, 68

W

War Crimes Museum, 64
War veterans, 116c
Water buffaloes, 11c, 96c
Waterfalls, 73c
Water-puppet performances, 128
Westmoreland, Gen. William, 45c, 46
White Silk Lake, 106
Woodcarving, 128
World War II, 38

X

Xa Loi Pagoda, 61, 61c
Xe dap loi carts, 11c
Xich lo transport, 58c
Xuan Hoang Lake, 73c

Y

Yellow Wall, 90c

Z

Zao people, 123c
Zodiac, 131
Zoos, 64c

136 Customs change quickly, but the bicycle remains the most common means of transportation, especially in northern Vietnam.

Map: Patrizia Derossi

ILLUSTRATION CREDITS

Archivio White Star: pages 28 top, 28-29, 29 top left, 29 top right, 29 bottom right.

Antonio Attini / Archivio White Star: pages 54 top left, 54 top right, 55 top, 55 centre, 55 bottom, 57, 56-57, 59, 58 top right, 60-61, 61 top left, 61 bottom left, 61 top right, 61 bottom right, 65, 64 top left, 64 centre left, 64 bottom left, 64 right, 72 top left, 72 top right, 72-73, 73 top right, 73 bottom right, 73 bottom left, 76 top right, 77 top right, 78 top left, 88 top right, 89 bottom right, 91-94, 104 top right, 107 top right, 108 top left, 108 bottom left, 109 top left, 109 top right, 116 bottom right, 115, 119 bottom left, 124 bottom left, 126 left, 126 right, 127 left, 127 top right, 128 bottom left, 128 top left, 128 top right, 128 bottom right, 128-129, 130 top right.

Agenzia Gamma: pages 40 centre, 42 centre left.

Agenzia Visa: pages 38 bottom right, 41 top, 41 centre, 41 bottom, 42 top left, 42 bottom left.

Akg Photo: pages 34 bottom left, 36 top, 36 centre, 36 bottom, 39 top left, 39 top right, 44 left, 44 centre, 46 top, 46 centre, 46 bottom, 48 top, 48 bottom, 49, 50 bottom, 51 top.

F. Barbagallo: pages 58 left, 58 bottom right.

P. Baudry / Visa: page 110 top left.

C. Boisvieux: pages 1, 8 top, 9 top, 62-63, 70 top, 74 top left, 74 top right, 76 top left, 78 top right, 78-79, 79 top right, 79 bottom right, 84 bottom left, 89 top right, 97, 98 top right, 98 top left, 98-99, 100-101, 103 centre right, 106 bottom, 108-109, 110 bottom left, 116 top left, 119 top right 119 bottom right, 121, 124 top left, 131 top right.

C. Boisvieux / Hémispheres: pages 2-7 foreground, 90 top, 98 bottom right, 123 top left.

Bill Cardoni / Agenzia Speranza: page 110 bottom right.

Nicolas Cornet: pages 8 bottom 8-9, 10 top left, 26 top right, 26 bottom left, 38 top left, 38 top right, 40 top, 40 bottom, 42 bottom right, 42 top right, 45 bottom left, 47 centre, 50 top, 52 right, 52 top left, 52 bottom left, 53 top left, 53 bottom left, 53 top right, 53 bottom right, 68-69, 76-77, 89 centre right, 95 top, 96 bottom left, 104 top left, 106-107, 113 top right, 114 left, 114-115, 122 top left, 124 bottom left, 131 bottom right.

Giancarlo Costa / Agenzia Stradella: pages 32 top left, 32 bottom left, 32 right, 35 top.

M. Cristofori / Sie: pages 110 top right, 116.

Jean Leo Dugast / The Stock House: pages 69 top left, 86-87, 88-89, 98 bottom left, 122-123, 125.

Mary Evans Picture library: page 33.

Stephane Frances / Hémispheres: pages 75 top right, 81 centre right, 81 bottom right, 130-131.

Patrick Frilet / Hémispheres: pages 86 top left, 87 right top.

Bertrand Gardel / Hémispheres: pages 10 top right, 11 top, 56 top right, 80-81, 79 top right, 86 bottom left, 136.

S. Grandadam: pages 112 top, 127 bottom basso, right.

Tim Hall: pages 75 bottom 103 bottom right, 105 top right, 104-105, 106 top, 124 top right, 130 top left.

Suzanne Held: pages 88 top left, 111, 116 top right, 123 bottom left.

Johner / Gamma: page 51 bottom.

Kharbine / Tapabor Collection: page 34 top left, 34 centre left.

Jean Kugler Photos / The Stock House: pages 56 top left, 102 top.

Laurent / Agenzia Gamma: page 45 right.

A. Lorgnier / Visa: pages 18-19, 69 top right.

S. Nardulli / Panda Photo: pages 74-75, 84-85.

Photobank: pages 2-7 background, 3-6, 10-11, 12 top right, 12 bottom right, 12 top left, 12 bottom left, 13, 16-17, 66 left, 66 right, 67 top left, 67 bottom left, 67 right, 68 bottom, 77 bottom right, 82, 83 bottom left, 83 top left, 83 bottom right, 83 top right, 87 top left, 90 bottom, 95 bottom, 96 bottom right, 102-103.

A. Pinsard / Visa: pages 122 top right, 123 right.

P. Ragazzini / Sie: page 84 top left.

Renault / Rieger / Gamma: pages 107 top left, 113 centre right.

Philippe Renault / Gamma: pages 54-55.

Roberto Rinaldi: page 68 top.

Roger Viollet: pages 26 top left, 34-35, 37 top left, 37 top right, 37 bottom left, 37 bottom right, 39 bottom right, 43 top left, 43 bottom left, 43 top right, 43 centre right, 53 bottom right, 45 top left.

Guido Rossi / The Image Bank: pages 47 bottom, 56 bottom left, 70 bottom, 70-71, 69 top, 84 centre left, 96 top right, 103 top right, 112-113, 113 bottom right, 119 top left, 120 top left.

Ben Simmons / The Stock House: page 58 right centre.

Taylor / Frabricius / Liaison / Gamma: page 11 bottom.

Steve Taymer / Black Star / Grazia Neri: pages 105 bottom right, 115 top, 116 bottom left, 120 top right, 120 bottom left, 120 bottom right.

The Bettman Archive: page 47 top.

Jack Urwiller / Barnaby's Picture Library: page 44 right.